W9-CTI-979

CITIZEN
13660

CITIZEN 13660

DRAWINGS AND TEXT BY

Miné Okubo

*With a new introduction
by Christine Hong*

UNIVERSITY OF WASHINGTON PRESS

Seattle & London

Design by Thomas Eykemans
Composed in Klinic Slab, typeface design by Joe Prince
17 16 15 14   5 4 3 2 1

UNIVERSITY OF WASHINGTON PRESS
PO Box 50096, Seattle, WA 98145-5096, U.S.A.
www.washington.edu/uwpress

LIBRARY OF CONGRESS CATALOGING-IN-PUBLICATION DATA
Okubo, Miné.
    Citizen 13660 / drawings and text by Miné Okubo ;
    with a new introduction by Christine Hong.
        p.   cm.
    Originally published: New York : Columbia University Press, 1946.
    Includes bibliographical references.
    ISBN 978-0-295-99392-8 (hardback) —
    ISBN 978-0-295-99354-6 (paperback)
1. Okubo, Miné.
2. Japanese Americans—Evacuation and relocation, 1942–1945.
3. World War, 1939–1945—Concentration camps—Utah.
4. Tanforan Assembly Center (San Bruno, Calif.)
5. Central Utah Relocation Center.
6. World War, 1939–1945—Personal narratives, American.
I. Title.
    D769.8.A6O38 2014
    940.54'72730979469—dc23
    [B]   2013042720

The paper used in this publication is acid-free and meets the minimum requirements of American National Standard for Information Sciences—Permanence of Paper for Printed Library Materials, ANSI Z39.48–1984.∞

To the memory of my mother

Introduction

Christine Hong

OVER half a century after being forced by wartime government directive to leave her Berkeley home, Miné Okubo, on the occasion of the Day of Remembrance, February 19, 1993, would reflect on the legacy of the mass removal and incarceration of 120,000 ethnic Japanese in the United States, the majority of whom were citizens like her.[1] By then in her eighties, the California-born Japanese American artist, chiefly recognized for *Citizen 13660* (1946), an illustrated memoir of life behind barbed wire and under armed guard, remarked on time's corrosive consequences. Nowhere were these effects more poignantly apparent than in the deaths of "more than two-thirds of the evacuees."[2] "To know what it was like," Okubo asserted of the world-shattering experience of the camps, "one would have had to live the shock, humiliation, loss, misery, sorrows and tears."[3] Yet, several decades after Franklin Roosevelt's signing of Executive Order 9066, which authorized the displacement of people of Japanese ancestry from the western United States

into hastily erected "relocation centers," Okubo would comment that all "ten camps are gone."[4] Eroded by the elements, the physical edifices of the camps—partly constructed through the labor of those imprisoned inside who had "helped to finish the barracks and even helped to build the barbed wire fences"—were, in Okubo's estimation, too scantily commemorated by "stone memorial monuments."[5] As she nonetheless observed, only these isolated memorials, inscribed "with few things representative of each camp, remain to make the camps sights."[6]

Yet "mak[ing] the camps sights"—by bringing into view "the shock, humiliation, loss, misery, sorrows and tears" of those incarcerated within—is precisely the project that has defined Okubo's own legacy. With its nearly two hundred line drawings exposing "what happens to people when reduced to one status and condition," *Citizen 13660* visualized the American concentration camp experience with striking thoroughness of coverage.[7] Heralded by Okubo herself, always a vigorous promoter of her own work, as "the first inside-the-camp documentary story of the Japanese evacuation and internment," *Citizen 13660* granted outsiders rare access to scenes of everyday life within camp confines.[8] As Okubo would explain in the preface to the 1983 University of Washington Press reissue of her 1946 memoir, "Cameras and photographs were not permitted in the camps, so I recorded everything in sketches, drawings, and paintings." Prohibited access to those modes of media technology endowed with evidentiary weight, Okubo, according to her own spirited account, made recourse to the drawn medium as an alternative means of record. In less than two years' time, in her self-appointed role as "observer and reporter," Okubo would remarkably generate a vast wartime oeuvre of over two thousand portraits of camp life, rendered in a range of styles and media, including ink, watercolor, charcoal, tempera, and gouache.[9] Given the sheer scale of this output, it is no surprise that others incarcerated at Tanforan Assembly Center in California and Topaz Relocation Center in Utah would recall Okubo always "with sketch-book in hand."[10] Of this image of Okubo as a dogged chronicler of camp life, poet Toyo Suyemoto would write, "I see you, as I remember Tanforan, recording scenes from camp life which culminated in your book, *Citizen 13660*."[11]

Insofar as *Citizen 13660* signaled an uncommon entry into cultural representation at a historical juncture in which the political rights of people of Japanese ancestry in the United States had been suspended, the conditions enabling its publication merit scrutiny. Particularly pertinent, here, is an inquiry into "what rhetorical strategies were available to the . . . racially proscribed non-citizen."[12] Relative to *Citizen 13660*, we might extend this question

to encompass the enemy alien, the disenfranchised citizen, and the collateralized human located on the home front of total war. Neither assuredly inside nor wholly outside the bounds of the imagined community of the United States, such subjects were submitted to a national security calculus, stripped of their rights to due process and effectively deemed by wartime authorities to be disloyal until proven loyal. A 1944 study of racial prejudice against Japanese Americans found that "virtually every person of Japanese descent in the United States has been thoroughly investigated."[13] Vulnerable to state power and deprived of mechanisms of self-governance, which could be summarily "dissolved" at any time by army order, the incarcerated, as Okubo put it, "were close to freedom yet far from it."[14] How, then, do we explain what appears to be the exceptionality of *Citizen 13660* as a sweeping visual record, by a "racially proscribed," dispossessed, and disenfranchised citizen, of a historical event "designed not to be seen"?[15] Given the off-limits settings of the camps—strategically removed as they were from ordinary view—how might we account, moreover, for the memoir's explicit "exhibition purposes"?[16]

As Okubo would colorfully narrate to younger generations of scholars interested in researching her wartime oeuvre, *Citizen 13660*, in its publication by Columbia University Press in 1946, had appeared "too soon after the war," when "anything Japanese was still rat poison."[17] Yet Okubo's thesis on the supposed prematurity of *Citizen 13660* in its immediate postwar appearance neglects both the thorny early reception history of the memoir and her instrumental role, throughout her long career, in framing its social and political meaning. Indeed, Okubo's assiduous curation of the significance of *Citizen 13660*, long after the last camp was shuttered and her camp memoir first published, should alert us to the fact that the leitmotif of what she, in later years, referred to as "the internment" remained for her an active site of construction and meaning making.[18] Even, this is to say, as "the breadth and immensity of the paintings she produced in the last fifty years of her life" have garnered meager critical attention, any attempt to periodize Okubo's body of work neatly into camp and postcamp phases is complicated by her recurrent efforts to condition the meaning of her memoir.[19] Indeed, much as Okubo originally captioned the line drawings in Citizen 13660 with framing text, so too would she thereafter endeavor to frame the camp experience, through paratextual and extratextual commentary, for successive generations of her readers.

Particularly crucial to the afterlife of Citizen 13660 was Okubo's own political evolution with regard to the camps. Daring to go "back again," as she put it, by embracing "her Japanese heritage," Okubo, in the late 1960s and 1970s, would turn to primitivist aesthetics in her artwork.[20] In this era of dawning yellow power consciousness, she would no longer find it possible to consider herself "a full American," a startling claim that appears in the catalogue for her solo retrospective 1972 show at the Oakland Museum.[21] "The Evacuation demonstrated that other Americans considered her an alien," the catalogue reads, "because her race was yellow."[22] Confronted with the spectacle of US hot war in Asia during this juncture, Okubo would detect in the plight of Vietnamese refugees echoes of her own wartime camp experience.[23] Executed in the brooding smudge and lash of charcoal and the imprecision of gouache, the abstractly stylized camp portraits exhibited at the Oakland Museum, images not circulated for mass consumption at mid-century, would disclose contours of suffering and despair, a "pervasive gloom" not always tangible in the comics-style line drawings collected in Citizen 13660.[24] Yet in no way signaling a pessimistic break with her 1946 memoir, this era would see Okubo tirelessly pursue its republication, seeking to reanimate its significance for new generations of readers. Indeed, as the 1980s dawned, Okubo's involvement in the Japanese American redress movement would naturalize a powerful retroactive interpretive lens for Citizen 13660. In 1981, two years before the University of Washington Press reissue of her book, Okubo testified before the Congress-sponsored Commission on Wartime Relocation and Internment of Civilians (CWRIC). Calling for "an apology and . . . reparation . . . in order to prevent [mass removal and incarceration] from happening to others," Okubo presented the CWRIC with a copy of her illustrated first-person memoir as apparently plain evidence of government wrongdoing. Okubo's remarks before the CWRIC would serve as a draft for her preface to the reissue of Citizen 13660, a paratextual framing that has conditioned contemporary interpretation of her memoir.[25] If ahead of its time in 1946, Citizen 13660 had, it would appear, come of age in an era of redress struggle. Initially published by an East Coast academic press a year after the war's end, Okubo's memoir would return to the West Coast in its 1983 reissue. More generally reflective of historiographical shifts in scholarship on the camps and mainstream consensus as to their injustice, Citizen 13660 is today typically read as a subtle yet discerning exposé of racist unfreedom at the heart of American democracy. Distinguished with an American Book Award in 1984 by the Before Columbus Foundation,

Citizen 13660 is routinely taught as part of a US postwar multicultural literary canon. Held out as a stark example of the costs of state-sponsored racialization, Okubo's account of camp life has been "assimilated by latter-day critics into the protest tradition," with her "words and images [construed] as weapons of resistance."[26]

We should be cautious, however, of naturalizing *Citizen 13660* within the trajectory of the redress movement. Against framings of *Citizen 13660* as before its time, a reading Okubo actively encouraged, we might ask how this illustrated chronicle, as the earliest published Japanese American narrative of the camps, was profoundly of its time. Far more difficult for contemporary readers to grasp is how Okubo's images of life behind barbed wire were perversely mobilized, in the transwar years, as an affirmation of the democratic potential of the American concentration camp. Neither a furtively realized project nor a threatening one—as Dorothea Lange's impounded War Relocation Authority (WRA) photographic record was deemed to be—Okubo's documentary project elicited keen interest from WRA officials.[27] In internal WRA and Bureau of Indian Affairs records, Okubo was singled out as one of a handful of "young people in the evacuee group" endowed with "special abilities and talents" regarded as valuable for "all the projects" ("projects" being the WRA euphemism for "camps").[28] Not only were Okubo's illustrations and writings for *Trek*, the Topaz literary journal, scrutinized by WRA officials prior to publication and assessed as "definitely loyal" in classified leave-clearance documents, but also her intention to "write a book [based] on her experiences here" was favorably acknowledged by the WRA officials who cleared her for "resettlement" eastward, in New York.[29] As historian

Greg Robinson points out, "Okubo's work was promoted by the [WRA], the government agency responsible for running the camps, and its liberal allies outside of government, as part of a larger program of assimilation and absorption they had designed for the Nisei."[30] Okubo, Robinson states, "collaborated in this operation, not only in her choice of illustrations for [*Citizen 13660*], and in the brief texts she wrote to accompany them, but in her various public statements characterizing herself as a writer."[31] Perhaps unsurprisingly, then, "former jailers of the Japanese Americans" were among the early enthusiastic chorus of reviewers who acclaimed *Citizen 13660*'s democratic value.[32] From Dillon Myer, head of the WRA from 1942 to 1946 and the Bureau of Indian Affairs from 1950 to 1953, and therefore "director and commissioner of twin calamities," *Citizen 13660* elicited this remarkable endorsement: "This book is a reproof to those who would malign any racial minority, and it should help to forestall any future mass movements of the type [Okubo] portrays."[33]

In its early reception, *Citizen 13660* garnered an impressive body of laudatory response from an elite spectrum of liberal voices, including camp officials, prominent critics of government policy toward people of Japanese ancestry, and renowned Asia authorities. Whatever their radically varying degrees of individual liability for the roundup, mass removal, and indiscriminate incarceration of people of Japanese ancestry from the western United States—indeed, some had none—WRA chief Dillon Myer, WRA public relations head M. M. Tozier, Nobel laureate and China "expert" Pearl Buck, *Survey Graphic* literary critic Harry Hansen, progressive writer Carey McWilliams, and *Common Ground* editor

M. Margaret Anderson offered strikingly converging assessments of *Citizen 13660* as an unvarnished historical record by an unimpeachably American artist.[34] Curiously, the value of Okubo's representation of the camps, which its postwar reviewers amply affirmed, was forecast in an early 1942 report, "On the Japanese Question in the United States," submitted by lieutenant commander K. D. Ringle to the WRA and published anonymously in abridged form in the October 1942 issue of *Harper's Magazine*. Generated prior to the authorization of the mass removal of West Coast ethnic Japanese, this report contended "that the nisei could be accorded a place in the national war effort without risk or danger," and it offered policy prescriptions toward this end.[35] To thwart any possible public conception of "the relocation centers and the evacuees . . . [as] laboratory specimens," a function of the camps that, if plainly broadcast, would surely arouse resentment, Ringle advised WRA officials to promote "a history of the entire evacuation and resettlement program from the point of view of those affected," pointing to the ideological value of an account "with accompanying pictorial illustrations."[36] As their contribution to "the national war effort," Ringle explained, representation by the incarcerated of their camp experience "would go farther than anything else toward committing their loyalty to the United States."[37]

To be clear, I do not mean to suggest that *Citizen 13660* was scripted or co-opted in advance by government authorities and their cadre of experts, much less to insinuate a straightforward genealogical trajectory between the Ringle report and Okubo's illustrated memoir. Nor do I intend to imply that the meaning of Okubo's narrative was congealed in its fraught early reception,

which praised the retrospective narration of camp life "by an evacuee, some one who actually saw, felt, and was part of this amazing adventure."[38] Rather I wish to highlight the fact that Nisei self-representation was among the "arsenal of technologies" explicitly discussed by camp officials "for managing [Japanese Americans] during wartime" and after their release from camp confinement.[39] This is to say that the publication of *Citizen 13660* so soon after the war was contingent on a nexus of structural factors, including WRA support, that complicate its recovery as a self-evident critique of government wrongdoing. Even as one postwar reviewer after another commented upon moments of irony or wry critique in *Citizen 13660*—when Okubo reports, for example, "Letters from my European friends told me how lucky I was to be free and safe at home"—the early reception of Okubo's account of camp life was not defined by demands for government accountability, nor was her work seen as leaning in that direction.[40] Rather, more worthy of note is the curious continuum between liberal critic and liberal administrator of the camps. Insisting on the "entirely American" character of *Citizen 13660* and emphasizing Okubo's "acute American mind," even someone like Pearl Buck, who had on numerous occasions spoken out against US government policy toward its ethnic Japanese minority, would assess Okubo's memoir in language that, in both tone and substance, would uncannily echo the content of letters from "Caucasian" character references in Okubo's WRA file.

Insofar as these confidential letters aimed to furnish intelligence on Okubo in order to better equip WRA authorities to evaluate her application for leave clearance (infamously also known as the "loyalty questionnaire"), these and other documents in Okubo's "evacuee case file" demand to be critically read against the grain of their narrow securitized focus. They also merit comparative consideration against the early reception of *Citizen 13660* in order to retrieve their shared logic with the early reviews of Okubo's work. Indeed, the homology between the reviews of *Citizen 13660* and the informant evaluations of Okubo as "Citizen 13660" is striking. On multiple discursive registers—Okubo's memoir, the postwar reviews of her memoir, and her late-war leave-clearance process—the fraught twofold task at hand was not only to Americanize the camp experience but also to redomesticate the alienized camp inmate. Implicitly at risk in this process was no less than the stability of American democracy itself. In the main, the letters collected in Okubo's "Internal Security report" anticipated and comported with this recuperative logic, vouching for the artist's loyalty and utter Americanness while disavowing the deleterious effects of the camp as a massively unjust carceral system. "In answer to your inquiry concerning Mine [*sic*] Okubo," Glenn Wessels strenuously maintained in his letter to WRA director Dillon Myer that "all [Okubo's] ties are with America and that she has few important associations with Japan and with people of Japanese blood."[41] Referencing Okubo's supposed penchant for the society of "American, not Japanese artists," Wessels, a former Works Progress Administration (WPA) supervisor under whom Okubo had worked in the early war years, took his argument for her release further: "I have known a number of Japanese and Japanese American artists, but I do not know of any that was so un-Japanese in sympathies and in manner of thought as Mine [*sic*] Okubo."[42] John Haley, who taught Okubo at the University of California,

Berkeley, where she received her bachelor's degree in 1935 and her master's degree in fine arts in 1936, would, in similarly ringing terms, provide an endorsement of his former student as "thoroughly American in thought and training and . . . loyal to American ideals."[43]

All told, the "Loyalty and Character" section of Okubo's WRA file would entail the agency's communication with at least five references, including a former landlady, an ex-classmate, and three art teachers; the confirmation of biographical details that had been volunteered by Okubo on her application for leave clearance; and the collation of any local police and federal agency files on her. It would also insidiously require testimony, from unnamed camp "informants," on the question of Okubo's loyalty. Okubo would elliptically reference this exit process in *Citizen 13660*. "I was photographed," reads the caption below an image of "Okubo," Okubo's comic self-figuration, whose face is now fixed within the parameters of a frame for the purpose of generating a mug shot for her case file. That "Okubo" must be photographically captured as a condition of the WRA exit process points to a seamless logic linking the state's indiscriminate framing of her and other ethnic Japanese as "enemy aliens," which legitimated the establishment of the camps in the first place, to the intelligence-gathering surveillance mechanisms through which she and others were forced to pass in order to secure leave from the camps.[44] In comments accompanying a tableau toward the end of her memoir, Okubo describes the intensity of "red tape" in the leave clearance–cum–loyalty determination process, with applicants "checked and double checked and rechecked" by WRA officials.[45] Citizens like her, she states, "were asked to swear unqualified allegiance to the United States and to defend it faithfully from all foreign powers."[46] As Okubo's WRA records demonstrate, in response to the prompt "Have you ever applied for repatriation to Japan?" she would supplement her "no" (all that was required) with a handwritten comment, "I owe my allegiance to the United States of America."[47] Indeed, Okubo counted herself as a member of the "Other Residents of Topaz," a group of self-professed "loyal American citizens" who sought to avow to camp and other federal authorities that their "loyalty to [their] country is something to be expressed without reference to past grievances or wounds."[48] Okubo would add her signature to a collective statement that declared unconditional loyalty to the point of death: "We shall register, we are loyal, we shall fight for the United States." What goes undisclosed in *Citizen 13660*'s closing lines is that, on her leave-clearance forms, the artist listed propaganda work, specifically "Defense Work—war posters, moral[e] posters (creative painting mural work)," as her primary choice for postcamp employment.[49]

Here, it is worth considering that liberal multiculturalism, as an early Cold War mode of racial knowledge, did "not just arrange human beings along a pregiven scale of value."[50] Rather, it "secured specific historical configurations of personhood, . . . as possible, imaginable, and sustainable."[51] At stake in the early postwar reception of *Citizen 13660* was less Okubo's ability, as author, to unidirectionally will the postwar rehabilitation of the Nisei citizen-subject as an American subject—an impossible task given the countervailing, alienizing forces exerted on the latter by the wartime US national security state. Instead, *Citizen 13660* set into motion a dynamic of readerly identification and empathy that merits consideration in its own right. What we recover when we examine the memoir's postwar reception history is the striking renaturalization of the Nisei as a bona fide "American" subject—not by dint of training in "forums on 'How to Make Friends' and 'How to Behave in the Outside World'" or even necessarily because of that subject's performative identification as 100 percent American.[52] Rather, the dynamic of postwar readerly empathy, of "Caucasian" identification with "Citizen 13660," was central to the ex post facto democratic inclusion and recognition of the Nisei as an American citizen. A September 26, 1946, review of the memoir, "Concentration Camp, U.S. Model," offers a representative leveling argument: "All Americans are members of minorities. Almost all of these minorities have at one time or another, here or elsewhere, been fractioned off and persecuted." The review concludes, "We should all join with Miss Okubo, therefore, when she recalls: 'A feeling of uncertainty hung over the camp; we were worried about the future.'"[53] As a crucial vehicle for "white Americans . . . to get to know difference," postwar cultural texts enabled them "to learn the supposed inside stories of people of color."[54] Along these very lines, it is worth considering the stunning claim, advanced by the former public relations chief of the WRA M. M. Tozier, that *Citizen 13660* vicariously and anachronistically granted him his most palpable entry into "camp life": "After reading this book, I felt that I knew for the first time what camp life looked like, smelled like, and felt like to the evacuated people."[55] Not only had the camps "actually happened," but also, as Tozier sweepingly declared, they "might have happened to you."[56] Fostered through the conceit of empirical access and the fiction of firsthand knowledge, readerly empathy thus enabled the postwar domestication of the camp experience as an emphatically American story. And it did so by heralding the national identity between "Caucasians" outside camp and "Japanese" inside barbed-wire enclosures, erasing meaningful structural differences in the process. In other words, by dematerializing the conditions that gave rise to the racist mass roundup and incarceration of ethnic Japanese in the United States, postwar empathy on the part of Citizen 13660's readers enabled the ideological recovery of "American" national identity on shared "human" grounds. Indeed, as the editor of Common Ground sought to prevail upon Okubo while she was still imprisoned at Topaz, her account of the camp—no longer strictly a "Japanese" story—should above all highlight "the very human situations in which the evacuees find themselves" as a way of fixing the fact that "we all have so much more in common than we have in differences."[57] Postwar public acceptance of "the evacuees," as WRA chief Myer likewise argued in a Common Ground article, was vital to the potential of the "relocation" as a democratic experiment.[58] Yet the fact that "common ground" with "the evacuees" was the anticipated ideological effect of readerly engagement with Citizen 13660 might give us some pause insofar as it signaled a genre shift away from the racial logic of the war-era "funnies" that Okubo so loved to read.

Hailed in its first appearance as a "graphic report" and "documentary drawing at its finest," Citizen 13660 invites comparison not only with the documentary camera image but also with the comics form.[59] Far from neutral ground, the drawn medium was itself the site of dueling propaganda during the Pacific War. On the US home front, the Japanese, cast in a variety of racist tropes—as buck-toothed, bespectacled Tojos; massified faceless hordes; monkeys, apes, and other simian creatures; and infestations of vermin or encroaching octopi—were also rendered as "fifth-column" figures by no less a beloved cartoonist than Dr. Seuss (Theodor Geisel).[60] Superman, for its part, ran a two-month storyline in mid-1943 that featured its titular hero going undercover in a WRA relocation camp "by contorting his super-facial muscles . . . [to] look like a Jap," a strip denounced by some in the public as "inciting race hatred."[61] All this underscores the fact that the wartime "construction of Japanese Americans as an internal enemy was itself partly a visual process. A demeaning caricature of the Japanese face was imprinted on the public through posters, graffiti, atrocity films, cartoons, and caricatures."[62] The ubiquity of these mass-mediated xenophobic images registers as an anxiety-inducing thematic in the opening, pre-removal section of Citizen 13660. Several scenes cast "Okubo" in despondent encounters with various media—reading newspapers, listening to the radio, and scrutinizing a publicly posted government order. In one connotatively dense image, a weary and sickened "Okubo," with arms outstretched across a newspaper, is bombarded by floating jingoistic headlines, race-baiting slogans, "Jap Crow" signs, and racist graffiti: "Sorry No Japs," "Enemy Planes Off Coast," "Send Them Back to Tojo," "Dangerous Criminals," "A Jap Is a Jap," to list a few. Theories of the nation as an "imagined community" fostered through print capitalism enable us to understand only part of the story that Okubo wishes to tell.[63] Shadowing the word-image combinations in Citizen 13660 is the history of American comics as a racializing technology. In the top right-hand corner of the portrait of the betwixt and between "Okubo"—hailed simultaneously as the "us" (citizen) and the "them" (enemy) of the wartime nation—is a crudely drawn slant-eyed face adorned with the caption "A Jap Looks Like This."[64] Neither solely an effect of print capitalism nor, for that matter, a result of formal citizenship status, the imagined community of the United States in the context of World War II as a total war was consolidated, this scene reveals, against the alien image of the "Jap." Insofar as racist caricature interpellates members of the nation into imagined unity, the cartoon vernacular of the "Jap," as the constitutive exclusion of the wartime United States, leaves "Okubo" precariously located on the unassimilated border of the nation, neither inside nor outside.

It is, moreover, precisely Okubo's formal figuration of "Okubo" *as the border* that begins to disclose the complexity of *Citizen 13660*'s visual strategies of readerly solicitation and its shrewd reworking of the comics, or "funnies," form. Albeit not framed on four sides by straight black lines, nearly all of Okubo's images of camp life are bounded by her self-referential figuration of herself depicted in the act of viewing. Her side profile frames nearly every image of *Citizen 13660*—a strategy that anticipates the testimonial comics image of late-twentieth-century human rights graphic novels. As both historical eyewitness and transhistorical mediator of the scene before her, "Okubo" conveys a double-sided message: an authenticating, testimonial "I saw it" on the one hand, and an ideologically universalizing "this could be you" on the other. As a vehicle for us, "Okubo" serves as a transactional figure, facilitating the spatially and temporally removed reader's

vicarious access into the world of the camp. As with Nakazawa Keiji's Hiroshima manga *Barefoot Gen*, Art Spiegelman's Holocaust graphic narrative *Maus*, and Joe Sacco's human rights graphic journalism, the first-person historical witness in Okubo's *Citizen 13660*, namely, "Okubo," functions stylistically and symbolically as a border, as a mediator between asymmetrical social worlds, one deformed by risk and suffering, and the other conditioned by the security of distance. That "Okubo" straddles these two dimensions—that of the camp in the hidden interior of the United States and that of outside American society—without easily resolving into either one furthermore raises the question of what it ideologically means *to function as the border* within the securitized domestic context of total war. Liberty for all, as the story of the camps suggested, was premised on unfreedom for some.

Signaling both the material history of the wartime camps as a traumatic event that was specifically borne by people of Japanese ancestry in the United States and the theoretical possibility that such a system of unfreedom might eventually encompass the outside "Caucasian" viewer, the first-person subject of Okubo's memoir thus not only mediated but also mitigated the realities of wartime risk. In effect holding the gaze of the outside viewer, "Okubo"—as a historical eyewitness embedded within scenes of camp life—cannily worked as a framing device that solicited the meaning of the camps through the engagement of postwar readers. Two temporalities were at odds here: the nonsequential time of incarceration that challenged any progressive or recuperative reading of the camps versus the progressive time of a nation capable of moving past its "mistakes."[65] Central to the ascendancy of the latter temporality was the postwar dynamic of read-erly empathy.

This dynamic hinged on the "super-vision" of the post-war reader, whose interpretive frame at once aligned with and superseded that of "Okubo" as a situated meaning-making mechanism within *Citizen 13660*'s scenes of camp life.[66] Exteriorized within the field of vision, the autobi-ographical first-person subject, "I," whose perspective structures that of *Citizen 13660*'s outside viewer, is spa-tially rendered as "Okubo"—visualized, in third-person terms, as an object of perception. As both first-person vehicle and third-person object relative to the reader, "Okubo" signals less framed narrative than framed recep-tion. This is nowhere more pointedly represented than in Okubo's depiction of a prowling camp policeman. This scene stages "Okubo" in the act of spying on the police-man, who, in turn, is caught in the act of peering through a knothole at men gambling inside a barracks. If "Okubo" has hitherto served as our perspectival vehicle for entry into the camp, in this scene, we are confronted with a dis-comfiting doppelgänger of the intended outside viewer: namely, the "Caucasian" voyeur.[67] Highlighting the pruri-ence of the visual act, this image offers the layered com-mentary that seeing, relative to the historic context of internment, is a far from neutral activity. Essential to the regulation of camp life, viewing, as depicted in this scene, cannot be divorced from predatory state surveillance and the asymmetrical power relations that structure its range of possible meanings and potentially fateful reper-cussions. To the extent that speculations of fifth-column activity furnished a national security pretext for mass incarceration, this scene offers a rejoinder, at once allego-rizing the hysteria-prone wartime beholder and calling for critical disidentification on the part of the postwar reader. In Okubo's treatment, the "spy" is no Issei, Kibei, or Nisei in the subterranean employ of the Japanese emperor but rather the "Caucasian."

Indeed, as incommensurate modes of perception, spying and witnessing confront the reader with a democ-ratizing challenge. Insofar as "Okubo" and the "Cauca-sian" camp policeman function as proxies for the implied viewer beyond the frame, with their act of looking being the precondition for our access, the scene presents an intersubjective overture, in effect requesting the reader to intervene on behalf of one side or the other, to referee a contest of perspective as well as to declare affinities, if not empathy, with one of the viewers in the frame. Whimsically *Matryoshka*-like in visual architecture, the scene features literally captive subjects who, by engaging in the banned activity of gambling, command a "captive" but formally free audience in the figure of the "Cauca-sian" camp policeman, who unwittingly serves as the visual object of "Okubo," a captive but privileged viewer. Thereby visualizing the issue of reception, this scene queries less who will have the final word than who ulti-mately can claim the more all-encompassing view and whose reading will "frame" the others. By representing vying modes of apperception, this scene bespeaks Oku-bo's formal strategies to prompt the alignment of her viewer. An estranging portrait, not to mention a discom-fiting possible placeholder for the "Caucasian" reviewer of *Citizen 13660*, the "Caucasian" voyeur, whose figu-ration is clearly meant to repel, tests the limits of eth-nic identification on the part of Okubo's "non-evacuee" readership.[68] Granted the privilege of a sweeping out-side view, the reader of *Citizen 13660* is invited to enter each of the framed scenes via figured, historically placed surrogates, with "Okubo" as a recursive—and therefore stable—subjective marker. And it is precisely in our identification with "Okubo" that *Citizen 13660* could, both in the immediate wake of the war and today, be recuperated as an American story.

I would like to thank Paul Moores, the acquisitions librarian at Riverside City College, who generously facilitated my access, on multiple occasions, to the Miné Okubo Collection at Riverside City College (hereafter RCC).

1   The first "Day of Remembrance" program was held by Asian American activists in 1978 at Camp Harmony, the site of the former assembly center in Puyallup, Washington. On the number of ethnic Japanese mass incarcerated as a result of Executive Order 9066, the Commission on Wartime Relocation and Internment of Civilians (CWRIC) found that the "policy of exclusion, removal and detention was executed against 120,000 people without individual review." See Commission on Wartime Relocation and Internment of Civilians, *Personal Justice Denied: Report of the Commission on Wartime Relocation and Internment of Civilians* (Seattle: University of Washington Press, 1997), 3. Similarly, Roger Daniels writes, "On February 19, 1942, a 'day of infamy' as far as the Constitution is concerned, Franklin Roosevelt signed Executive Order 9066, which was the instrument by which just over 120,000 persons, two-thirds of them American citizens, were confined in concentration camps on American soil, in some cases for nearly four years." These people, Daniels elaborates, "were guilty of nothing other than being ethnically Japanese." See Roger Daniels, *Prisoners without Trials: Japanese Americans in World War II* (New York: Hill and Wang—Farrar, Straus and Giroux, 1993), 46.

2   Miné Okubo, personal statement, February 19, 1993, box 30, folder 13, Miné Okubo Collection, RCC.

3   Ibid.

4   Executive Order 9066 designated vast swaths of the western United States as "military areas . . . from which any or all persons may be excluded" and sanctioned military authorities and "all Executive Departments, independent establishments and other Federal Agencies, to assist . . . in carrying out this Executive Order, including the furnishing of military aid, hospitalization, food, clothing, transportation, use of land, shelter, and other supplies, equipment, utilities, facilities, and services"—in essence, concentration camps. See Franklin Roosevelt, Executive Order 9066, "Authorizing the Secretary of War to Prescribe Military Areas," February 19, 1942, online at http://www.ourdocuments.gov/doc.php?doc=74.

5   Okubo, personal statement, February 19, 1993, Miné Okubo Collection, RCC.

6   Ibid.

7   Okubo, "Preface to the 1983 Edition," *Citizen 13660* (Seattle: University of Washington Press, 1983), ix (in this edition, xxvi).

8   Okubo, letter to Steven Florio, CEO of *The New Yorker*, April 27, 1990, Miné Okubo Collection, RCC. Several decades after his involvement as an editor at Columbia University Press in the original 1946 publication of *Citizen 13660*, Harold Laskey would—as a literary agent with Moseley Associates—again advocate on Okubo's behalf to Donald Ellegood at the University of Washington Press, which reissued Okubo's memoir in 1983. In a letter to Ellegood dated March 11, 1983, Laskey described Okubo as "one of the best promoters of her book." See Harold Laskey, letter to Donald Ellegood, March 11, 1983, box 19, folder 67, Miné Okubo Collection, RCC.

9   Deborah Gesensway and Mindy Roseman, *Beyond Words: Images from America's Concentration Camps* (Ithaca, NY: Cornell University Press, 1987), 73. In "Portrait of an Artist," a December 1942 biographical sketch of Okubo published in the Topaz arts and literary magazine *Trek*, Jim Yamada describes Okubo's furious productivity: "Since evacuation, Mine [*sic*] has made from 1500 to 2000 rough sketches. Later she intends to develop some of them into finished paintings. Her last extended creative effort was at Tanforan when she completed approximately 50 paintings in a month." See Jim Yamada, "Portrait of an Artist," Trek 1, no. 1 (December 1942): 22. An April 1947 issue of *Mademoiselle* magazine furnished an updated account of the volume of artwork Okubo created while in camp: "Miné . . . was too much the artist to remain idle. Instead, she made capital of her camp experiences and produced some two thousand drawings objectively recording every detail of camp life." See Sono Okamura, "The Nisei Discover a Larger America," *Mademoiselle*, April 1947, 342.

10 Toyo Kawakami (née Suyemoto), letter to Miné Okubo, February 19, 1979, box 7, folder 21, Miné Okubo Collection, RCC.

11 Ibid.

12 Janet Lyon, *Manifestoes: Provocations of the Modern* (Ithaca, NY: Cornell University Press, 1999), 62.

13 Carey McWilliams, *Prejudice: Japanese Americans: Symbol of Racial Intolerance* (Boston: Little, Brown and Company, 1944), 299.

14 Okubo, *Citizen 13660*, 91, 81.

15 Marita Sturken, "Absent Images of Memory: Remembering and Reenacting the Japanese Internment," in *Perilous Memories: The Asia-Pacific War(s)*, ed. T. Fujitani et al. (Durham, NC: Duke University Press), 46.

16 Okubo, "Preface to the 1983 Edition," *Citizen 13660*, ix.

17 Gesensway and Roseman, *Beyond Words*, 74.

18 On the inaccuracy and inappropriateness of the term "internment" to describe the mass incarceration of Japanese Americans, despite its wide usage in the redress struggle, historian Roger Daniels clarifies "that 'internment' was an ordinary aspect of declared wars and referred to a legal process, described in United States statutes, to be applied to nationals of a country with which the United States was at war." Given that the majority of people incarcerated as a result of Executive Order 9066 were US citizens who were not nationals of Japan, "what happened to most of the West Coast Japanese Americans in 1942 . . . should not be described with a word describing a legal process." See Roger Daniels, "Words Do Matter: A Note on Inappropriate Terminology and the Incarceration of Japanese Americans," in *Nikkei in the Pacific Northwest: Japanese Americans and Japanese Canadians in the Twentieth Century*, ed. Louis Fiset and Gail M. Nomura (Seattle: University of Washington Press, 2005), 190.

19 Elena Tajima Creef, "Following Her Own Road: The Achievement of Miné Okubo," in *Miné Okubo: Following Her Own Road*, ed. Greg Robinson and Elena Tajima Creef (Seattle: University of Washington Press, 2008), 5. The catalogue for Okubo's 1972 Oakland Museum exhibit, *Miné Okubo: An American Experience*, divides her work into the following phases: "Growing Up," "A European Experience (1938–1940)," "Evacuation: 1942–1944," "Rediscovering the Self," and "Happy Period." See *Miné Okubo: An American Experience* (Oakland: Oakland Museum of California, 1972), 12–51.

20 Okubo as quoted by Shirley Sun in *Miné Okubo: An American Experience*, exhibition catalogue (Oakland: Oakland Museum of California, 1972), 41. Also see page 46.

21 Ibid.

22 Ibid.

23 In a typed personal statement dated May 14, 1975, Okubo writes that she is frequently asked whether the camps could "happen again," to which she offers the following response: "Yes, I do believe this can happen again as it is now happening to the South Vietnamese refugees, for the Establishment and the system won't change." See Okubo, personal statement, May 14, 1975, box 30, folder 14, Miné Okubo Collection, RCC.

24 Sun, *Miné Okubo*, 22.

25 For Okubo's statement before the Congressional Committee, see Okubo, "Statement of Miné Okubo before the Congressional Committee on Wartime Relocation and Internment (1981)," in *A Tribute to Miné Okubo*, ed. Greg Robinson and Elena Tajima Creef, special issue of *Amerasia Journal* 30, no. 2 (2004): 15–18. With regard to the relationship of *Citizen 13660* to the redress struggle, the opportunity presented itself in both directions. Writing as a literary agent to the University of Washington Press in 1983, Harold Laskey—who as a former editor at Columbia University Press had shepherded *Citizen 13660* to publication in 1946—even suggested that the CWRIC report could be "useful in publicity and promotion" of Okubo's memoir. See Harold Laskey, letter to Donald Ellegood, March 11, 1983, Miné Okubo Collection, RCC. For its part, the National Council for Japanese American Redress purchased copies of *Citizen 13660*, upon its 1983 reissue, in bulk "to sell . . . through [their] newsletter and other events." See William Hohri, National Council for Japanese American Redress (NCJAR) letter to Miné Okubo, September 24, 1983, box 9, folder 8, Miné Okubo Collection, RCC.

26 Greg Robinson, "Birth of a Citizen: Miné Okubo and the Politics of Symbolism," in Robinson and Creef, *Miné Okubo: Following Her Own Road*, 159.

27 See *Impounded: Dorothea Lange and the Censored Images of Japanese American Internment*, ed. Linda Gordon and Gary Y. Okihiro (New York: W. W. Norton, 2006).

28 Miles E. Cary memorandum to E. R. Fryer, August 25, 1942, Miné Okubo evacuee case file, record group 210, stack area 18W3, row 8, compartment 27, shelf 5, National Archives Building, Washington, DC.

29 "Loyalty and Character Report on Mine [*sic*] Okubo," September 23, 1943, Miné Okubo evacuee case file. Also see Evelyn K. Johnson, assessment of Miné Okubo, January 30, 1943, Miné Okubo evacuee case file.

30 Robinson, "Birth of a Citizen," 160.

31 Ibid.

32 Richard Drinnon, *Keeper of Concentration Camps: Dillon S. Myer and American Racism* (Berkeley: University of California Press, 1987), 225.

33 Ibid, xxvi. Also see "Excerpts from Comments on 'Citizen 13660' by Miné Okubo," Miné Okubo papers 1932–2009, collection 94, University of California, Riverside, Special Collections and Archives.

34 "Excerpts from Comments on 'Citizen 13660' by Miné Okubo," Miné Okubo papers 1932–2009.

35 K. D. Ringle, "On the Japanese Question in the United States," Miscellaneous WRA Publications, Office File of Commissioner John Collier, 1933–1945, Records of the Bureau of Indian Affairs, record group 75, stack area 11E-Z, row 30, compartment 9, shelf 5, National Archives Building, Washington, DC.

36 Ibid.

37 Ibid.

38 Carey McWilliams, "The Nisei Speak," *Common Ground*, June 1944, 61.

39 T. Fujitani, *Race for Empire: Koreans as Japanese and Japanese as Americans during World War II* (Berkeley: University of California Press, 2011), 21.

40 Okubo, *Citizen 13660*, 61.

41 Glenn A. Wessels, letter to Dillon Myer, February 3, 1943, Miné Okubo evacuee case file.

42 Ibid.

43 John Haley, letter to War Relocation Authority, February 12, 1943, Miné Okubo evacuee case file.

44 Okubo, *Citizen 13660*, 207. Technically, the term "enemy alien," which derives from the Enemy Alien Act of 1798, refers to a citizen of a country with which the United States is at war whose liberties may be restricted "without any individualized showing of disloyalty, criminal conduct, or even suspicion." As legal scholar David Cole points out, however, during "World War II, the government extended that logic to intern 110,000 persons of Japanese ancestry, about two-thirds of whom were U.S. citizens." See David Cole, "Enemy Aliens," *Stanford Law Review* 54 (May 2002), 953.

45 Okubo, *Citizen 13660*, 205.

46 Ibid.

47 "War Relocation Authority Application for Leave Clearance," January 4, 1943, Miné Okubo evacuee case file.

48 Fujitani, *Race for Empire,* 180.

49 "War Relocation Authority Application for Leave Clearance," January 4, 1943, Miné Okubo evacuee case file. Of her desire to participate in the defense effort, Okubo would later state, "The impact of evacuation is not on the material and physical. It is something far deeper. It is the effect on the spirit. What hurts most was the idea of being segregated and put away in a camp completely divorced from the national defense effort." As quoted in Sun, *Miné Okubo,* 36.

50 Jodi Melamed, *Represent and Destroy: Rationalizing Violence in the New Racial Capitalism* (Minneapolis: University of Minnesota Press, 2011), 12.

51 Ibid.

52 Okubo, *Citizen 13660*, 207.

53 Alfred McClung Lee, "Concentration Camp, U.S. Model," *Saturday Review*, September 28, 1946, 12.

54 Melamed, *Represent and Destroy*, xvi.

55 "Excerpts from Comments on 'Citizen 13660' by Miné Okubo," Miné Okubo papers, 1932–2009.

56 Ibid.

57 M. Margaret Anderson, *Common Ground* letter to Miné Okubo, April 7, 1943, box 3, folder 35, Miné Okubo Collection, RCC.

58 Dillon Myer, "Democracy in Relocation," *Common Ground*, December 1943, 48.

59 "Excerpts from Comments on 'Citizen 13660' by Miné Okubo," Miné Okubo papers, 1932–2009.

60 See John W. Dower, *War without Mercy: Race and Power in the Pacific War* (New York: Pantheon Books—Random House, 1986), 77–180.

61 Todd S. Munson, "'Superman Says You Can Slap a Jap!': The Man of Steel and Race Hatred in World War II," in *The Ages of Superman: Essays on the Man of Steel in Changing Times*, ed. Joseph J. Darowski (Jefferson, NC: McFarland, 2012), 9.

62 Linda Gordon, "Dorothea Lange Photographs the Japanese American Internment," *Impounded: Dorothea Lange and the Censored Images of Japanese American Internment*, ed. Linda Gordon and Gary Y. Okihiro (New York: W. W. Norton, 2006), 37.

63 In *Imagined Communities*, Benedict Anderson famously theorizes the nation as an imagined community. As he writes, "Print languages laid the bases for national consciousness. . . . Speakers of the huge varieties of Frenches, Englishes, or Spanishes, who might find it difficult or even impossible to understand one

another in conversation, became capable of comprehending one another via print and paper. In the process, they gradually became aware of the hundreds of thousands, even millions, of people in their particular language-field, and at the same time that *only those* hundreds of thousands, or millions, so belonged. These fellow-readers, to whom they were connected through print, formed, in their secular, particular, visible invisibility, the embryo of the nationally imagined community." See Benedict Anderson, "The Origins of National Consciousness," *Imagined Communities: Reflections on the Origins and Spread of Nationalism* (London: Verso, 1983), 44.

64 Okubo, *Citizen 13660*, 10.

65 Absent the orienting time markers in the text that accompanies the images in *Citizen 13660*, Okubo's memoir, on a purely visual register, is markedly nonlinear. Camp life, as Okubo notes, was "shiftless," and "a feeling of uncertainty" stifled all future prospects. See Okubo, *Citizen 13660*, 139. In this regard, *Citizen 13660* challenges the definition of comics as "sequential art," namely, Will Eisner's formulation as popularized by comics theorist Scott McCloud. The question, I would argue, is less whether Okubo's work comports with prevailing definitions of comics form than how *Citizen 13660*, as a visual narrative of mass confinement, troubles the progressive teleological assumptions and limitations of such definitions. On the definition of comics as sequential art, see Scott McCloud, *Understanding Comics: The Invisible Art* (New York: Kitchen Sink–HarperPerennial, 1994).

66 I borrow the term "super-vision" from Rey Chow's discussion of hegemonic US perception. See Rey Chow, "The Age of the World Target: Atomic Bombs, Alterity, Area Studies," in *The Age of the World Target: Self-Referentiality in War, Theory, and Comparative Work* (Durham, NC: Duke University Press, 2006), 39.

67 The term "Caucasian" was part of the War Relocation Authority lexicon. Below her image of a camp policeman spying on men gambling inside a barracks room, Okubo offers a translation in parentheses: "('Caucasian' was the camp term for non-evacuee workers.)." See Okubo, *Citizen 16330*, 60.

68 Ibid.

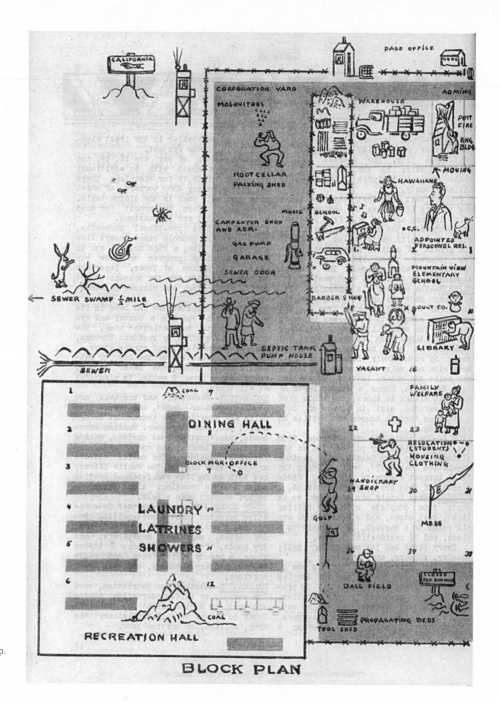

Miné Okubo, City of Topaz map.
Reproduced from *Trek* 1, no. 3
(June 1943): 18–19.

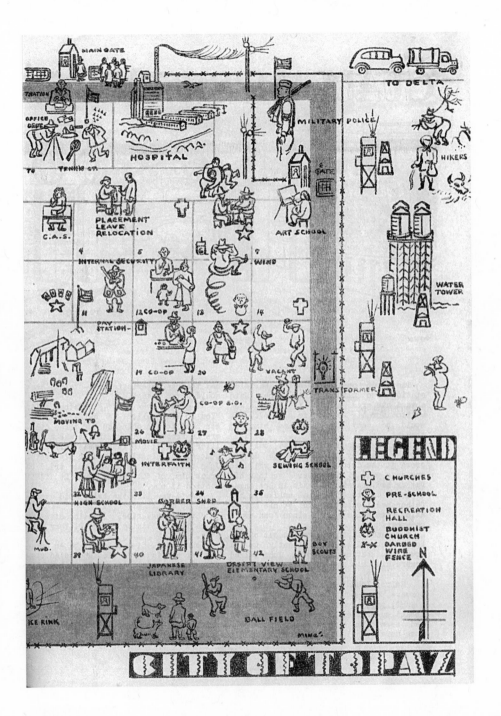

Preface to the 1983 Edition

FORTY-ONE years have passed since Pearl Harbor, the United States declaration of World War II, and the evacuation and internment of more than 110,000 people of Japanese descent—nearly two-thirds of them American citizens. Most of the first generation Issei and many of the second generation Nisei are deceased. All of the ten internment camps have disappeared in the remote desert and mountain areas where they were hurriedly built. The only surviving traces are pieces of concrete, pipes, and wire, and, in some of the camps, cemetery markers of the evacuees who died while in camp. Memorial monuments in stone have been erected in Manzanar and Tule Lake, and in other camps not so remotely removed. February 19, the day Executive Order 9066 was issued, has been named Remembrance Day by the Japanese Americans. Families and organizations make annual pilgrimages to keep the memory of the camp experience alive for the children, grandchildren, and great-grandchildren of the internees. The last camp had been closed in the spring of 1945, shortly before the end of the war.

Chinese and Japanese immigration to the United States took place principally on the West Coast, with the majority settling in California, and had a history marred by prejudice, hate, and economic fears. The Exclusion Act of 1924 had prohibited further immigration of people of Japanese descent and those already in the country were forbidden by law to become citizens, nor were they allowed to own property. In most parts of the country, little was known of the Japanese people in America.

After the attack on Pearl Harbor, the "yellow peril" hysteria was revived. The propaganda against the Japanese spread quickly across the country. President Franklin D. Roosevelt issued Executive Order 9066, ordering the mass evacuation from the West Coast and internment of all people of Japanese descent. The United States Army took charge. Within three weeks, race tracks, fair grounds, and parks were made over into assembly centers. Within three months, 110,000 people of Japanese parentage were moved from their homes. Later, they were sent to ten permanent camps: two in Arizona, two in Arkansas, two in California, and one each in Colorado, Idaho, Utah, and Wyoming. One camp, in Tule Lake, California, was for supposedly "disloyal" persons. Also the U.S. Department of Justice camps held 3,000 Japanese aliens considered potentially dangerous by the Federal Bureau of Investigation.

Incidentally, no cases of disloyalty were found in the camps. The Japanese Americans' part in the war effort in the Far East and the bravery and sacrifice of the much-honored 442nd Battalion of Japanese American soldiers proved further the loyalty to the United States of those of Japanese ancestry.

In the history of the United States this was the first mass evacuation of its kind, in which civilians were removed simply because of their race. Nothing had been prepared or planned for this rushed and forced evacuation. There were untold hardships, sadness, and misery.

At the time of the evacuation, I had just returned from two years of travel and study in Europe on a University of California/Berkeley Fellowship and was working on the Federal Arts Program doing mosaic and fresco murals commissioned by the United States Army. Although curfew was from 8:00 P.M. to 6:00 A.M. and we were not allowed to go beyond a five-mile radius of our home, I received a special permit to travel from Berkeley to Oakland so that I could finish the murals before being evacuated to Tanforan.

In the camps, first at Tanforan and then at Topaz in Utah, I had the opportunity to study the human race from the cradle to the grave, and to see what happens to people when reduced to one status and condition. Cameras and photographs were not permitted in the camps, so I recorded everything in sketches, drawings, and paintings. *Citizen 13660* began as a special group of drawings made to tell the story of camp life for my many friends who faithfully sent letters and packages to let us know we were not forgotten. The illustrations were intended for exhibition purposes.

I left camp when *Fortune* magazine asked me to come to New York to help illustrate the April 1944 issue on Japan. I then decided to make New York my home. In 1946 *Citizen 13660*, the first personal documentation of the evacuation story, was published by Columbia University Press.

Time mellows the harsh and the grim. I remember the ridiculous, the insane, and the humorous incidents and aspects of camp life. I was an American citizen, and because of the injustices and contradictions nothing made much sense, making things comical in spite of the misery. Crazy things were constantly happening in the camp, with close to ten thousand people confined in an area a mile square. There was no privacy. There was plenty of laughter in sharing discomforts, creating imaginative rumors and stories, and daydreaming wishful hopes. The different personalities and incidents come back to me often and I smile and wonder what happened to the poor souls.

After the war, California and the West Coast states were no longer restricted areas, and many of the evacuees who had relocated in the East and elsewhere now returned to build a new life. The close ties between Issei parents and Nisei children continued, only this time the parents were dependent upon their children. The Issei had lost their homes, businesses, farms, and everything they had struggled and suffered to build against the odds of prejudice, hate, and harassment, and most of them were too old to start again. After the war the Issei were at last given their rights to become citizens.

For the Nisei, evacuation had opened the doors of the world. After the war, they no longer had to return to the little Tokyos of their parents. The evacuation and the war had proved their loyalty to the United States.

The war was forgotten in the fifties. People throughout the country were busy rebuilding their lives. The country prospered and there were many signs of progress, including better communications generally and media far more open in their reporting. By 1960, however, when John F. Kennedy was elected president, imperfections in politics and elsewhere were quite apparent and young idealists were becoming aware of the many flaws and injustices in the Establishment. All the disastrous events—the Bay of Pigs fiasco, the Viet Nam war, the assassination of President Kennedy, and the sad plight of the Viet Nam veterans—led to the rebellious mood of the late sixties.

For the third generation Sansei, the children of Nisei parents, the seriousness of the evacuation had at first been difficult to comprehend, since many of them were born in the camps and others were born after the war and evacuation. By the 1970s, however, they were growing up and many were in college. When they understood what had happened to their parents and grandparents during World War II, they were incensed. They were very much concerned with all of the Asian countries and with Asian immigration to the United States. Asian studies centers were established first in colleges in the West and then nationwide. The Sansei became strongly organized and a force behind the redress movement to right the injustices suffered by Japanese Americans and to demand reparation for those evacuated and interned.

By this time the Nisei were in their prime, holding top positions in a variety of fields, including politics and government. (Today, we have a Nisei governor, two Nisei U.S. senators, two Nisei members of the House of Representatives, and mayors in several cities.) The Nisei were a well-organized group ready to bring to the world the injustice of the internment. From the mid-1970s through 1981, the story was spread widely in the news. Liberated minds of the time were interested, because generations of Americans did not know that this had ever happened in the United States to other American citizens. Books, articles, plays, exhibitions, television programs, and movies followed. Japanese Americans organized the redress movement to demand reparation for Japanese Americans and Alaskan Aleuts who had been forcibly removed from their homes and incarcerated in concentration camps.

Congress took measures to investigate the demands. The U.S. Commission on Wartime Relocation and Internment of Civilians was established in July 1980, and in 1981 ten public hearings were held in cities in the United States, including three in Alaska. Oral and written testimony was presented to the commission by many evacuees and others.

I testified at the hearing in New York City. As *Citizen 13660* had been widely reviewed and was considered an important reference book on the Japanese American evacuation and internment, I presented the commission with a copy of the book in addition to my oral testimony. In my testimony I stressed the need for young people from grade school through college to be educated about the evacuation. I believe that some form of reparation and an apology are due to all those who were evacuated and interned.

The Commission on Wartime Relocation and Internment is still active as this is written, and a report of its recommendations is expected early in 1983. The patient, tireless endeavor on the part of the Nisei and Sansei to right the wrong done during the war is commendable. The shocking story of the evacuation and internment of more than 110,000 people of Japanese descent is recorded for American history. The world now knows that this did happen in the United States.

I am often asked, why am I not bitter and could this happen again? I am a realist with a creative mind, interested in people, so my thoughts are constructive. I am not bitter. I hope that things can be learned from this tragic episode, for I believe it could happen again.

I wish to express my belated acknowledgment to Deborah Calkins, then with *Fortune* magazine, and Harold Laskey, then with Columbia University Press, for their assistance in making *Citizen 13660* possible.

MINÉ OKUBO
January 1983

CITIZEN 13660

WHEN England and France declared war on September 3, 1939, I had been traveling in Europe a year on an art fellowship from the University of California. I was stranded in Switzerland with nothing but a toothbrush. Everything that I owned was in Paris. The train fare from Budapest to Berne took my last cent and the money I had expected had not arrived at the American Express Office. Mail service was suspended and the French border was closed.

FORTUNATELY, I had friends living near Berne. After visiting around for a while, I ended up on a farm. Poland had been bombed and invaded, Switzerland feared invasion and all the men had been mobilized. As the situation grew steadily worse, my Swiss friends advised me to return home. I waited three months trying to arrange passage through France. A letter arrived from home saying that Mother was seriously ill. I decided to leave at once.

AT the French Consulate in Berne I learned that a transit visa to France would be given me if I secured a reservation on a boat sailing from a French port.

My Swiss friends loaned me the money for the boat fare. I sailed on the last boat leaving Bordeaux. It was crowded with refugees who told me vivid stories of their experiences.

I arrived in New York with exactly twenty-five cents, but collect telegrams fixed everything. I was soon safely home in California. However, the joy of my return was cut short by my mother's death.

Not long afterwards I found myself on the road again—this time to settle with a younger brother at Berkeley in the San Francisco Bay region.

I had a good home and many friends. Everything was
going along fine.

THEN on December 7, 1941, while my brother and I were
having late breakfast I turned on the radio and heard the
flash—"Pearl Harbor bombed by the Japanese!" We were
shocked. We wondered what this would mean to us and
the other people of Japanese descent in the United States.

OUR fears came true with the declaration of war against
Japan. Radios started blasting, newspapers flaunted scare
headlines.

ON December 11 the United States declared war on Germany and Italy. On the West Coast there was talk of possible sabotage and invasion by the enemy. It was "Jap" this and "Jap" that. Restricted areas were prescribed and many arrests and detentions of enemy aliens took place. All enemy aliens were required to have certificates of identification. Contraband, such as cameras, binoculars, short-wave radios, and firearms had to be turned over to the local police.

At this time I was working on mosaics for Fort Ord and for the Servicemen's Hospitality House in Oakland, California. I was too busy to bother about the reports of possible evacuation.

However, it was not long before I realized my predicament. My fellow workers were feeling sorry for me; my Caucasian friends were suggesting that I go East; my Japanese American friends were asking me what I would do if all American citizens and aliens of Japanese ancestry were evacuated. Letters from a sister in Southern California informed me that Father had been whisked away to an internment camp. A brother who was already in the army wrote letters full of wisecracks: "Better get ready for induction, kids. It's your turn now!"

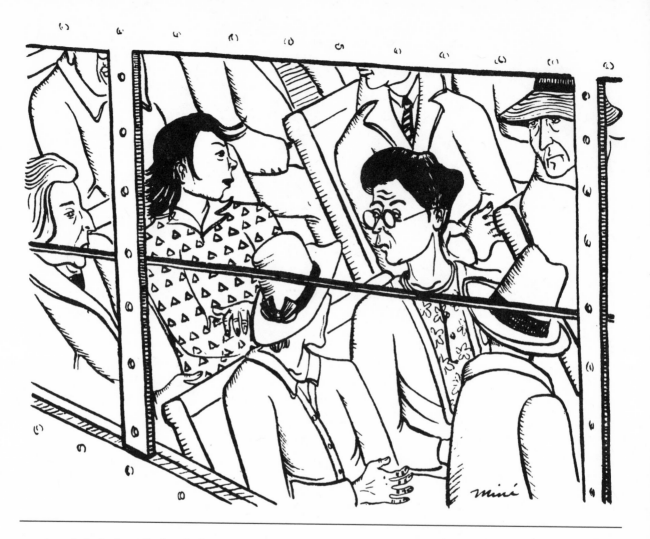

THE people looked at all of us, both citizens and aliens, with suspicion and mistrust.

On February 19, 1942, by executive order of the President, the enemy alien problem was transferred from the Department of Justice to the War Department. Restriction of German and Italian enemy aliens and evacuation of all American citizens and aliens of Japanese ancestry was ordered.

Public Proclamations Nos. 1 and 2 appeared in the newspapers. Three military areas were designated, including practically all of the coastal states of Washington, Oregon, and California, and the inland states of

Arizona, Idaho, Montana, Nevada, and Utah.

Evacuation was voluntary; people of Japanese ancestry were instructed to move out of the region on their own. Several thousand moved out of the vital coast areas but growing suspicion and general public antagonism caused unforeseen difficulties. On March 27, 1942, voluntary evacuation was halted and the army took over, to bring about a forced and orderly evacuation.

ON March 24, Public Proclamation No. 3 established the curfew. All American citizens and aliens of Japanese ancestry and other enemy aliens had to be home between the hours of 8 P.M. and 6 A.M. I had to have a special permit to travel to Oakland where I was employed because it was outside a five-mile radius of my home. Violation of any of the regulations meant fines and imprisonment.

The Federal Reserve Banks took charge of property owned by the evacuees, while the Farm Security Administration took over the agricultural property. This was necessary because of the social and economic vultures preying upon the unfortunates expecting to be evacuated.

"BE prepared for the Relocation Centers. Bring work clothes suited to pioneer life," was, in effect, one of the instructions. We made all kinds of hurried preparations. I had no difficulty finding boots and jeans but had to get friends to help find duffel bags, as most of the stores were sold out of them.

Shelter for 100,000 evacuees was constructed by the army within a space of three weeks. Race tracks and county fair grounds were changed overnight into assembly centers surrounded by military police and barbed wire. Fifteen centers were established, Manzanar in southern California being the first. Exclusion orders followed in rapid succession and the first formal mass evacuation started on March 31. Thousands were evacuated every day from the designated areas, and soon all American citizens and aliens of Japanese ancestry were moved from the entire state of California, the western half of Oregon and Washington, and the southern third of Arizona. In all, 110,000 were moved out; two thirds of them were native American citizens.

ON April 24, 1942, Civilian Exclusion Order No. 19 was issued and posted everywhere in Berkeley. Our turn had come.

We had not believed at first that evacuation would affect the Nisei, American citizens of Japanese ancestry, but thought perhaps the Issei, Japanese-born mothers and fathers who were denied naturalization by American law, would be interned in case of war between Japan and the United States. It was a real blow when everyone, regardless of citizenship, was ordered to evacuate.

CIVIL Control Stations were established by the Wartime Civil Control Administration in each of the designated areas. One member of each family was asked to register for the family; people without families registered individually. On Sunday, April 26, 1942, I reported to Pilgrim Hall of the First Congregational Church in Berkeley to register for my brother and myself—a family unit of two. Soldiers were standing guard at the entrance and around the buildings.

A woman seated near the entrance gave me a card with No. 7 printed on it and told me to go inside and wait. I read the "funnies" until my number was called and I was interviewed. The woman in charge asked me many questions and filled in several printed forms as I answered. As a result of the interview, my family name was reduced to No. 13660. I was given several tags bearing the family number, and was then dismissed. At another desk I made the necessary arrangements to have my household property stored by the government.

ON Tuesday when I returned to the Civil Control Station, I found our names posted on the board along with the family number. My family unit of two was scheduled to leave with the next to the last group at 11:30 A.M. on Friday, May 1, 1942. Our destination was Tanforan Assembly Center, which was at the Tanforan Race Track in San Bruno, a few miles south of San Francisco.

WE had three days and three nights to pack and get ready. My brother was excused from the University with a promise that he would receive his B.A. degree in June.

Our friends came to cheer us up and to wish us luck. It was like old home week but we were exhausted from work and worry. On the last morning the main part of the packing was finished but there was still plenty to be done. I asked different friends to take care of some of my cherished possessions. In the last hour I dashed to the bank to get some money, picked up my laundry, and paid my household bills.

WE tagged our baggage with the family number, 13660,
and pinned the personal tags on ourselves; we were
ready at last.

OUR friends came to take us to the Civil Control Station.
We took one last look at our happy home.

THE entire city block around the Civil Control Station was guarded by military police. Baggage was piled on the sidewalk the full length of the block. Greyhound buses were lined alongside the curb.

WE said good-bye to our friends and entered the Civil Control Station. Hundreds of evacuees were already there. A guide directed us to Group No. 4 to which we were assigned. Sandwiches and fruit were served by the church people.

At 11:30 A.M. Group 4 was called. We picked up our hand luggage and fell into line.

THE military police opened the bus door and we stepped into the bus as our family number was called. Many spectators stood around. At that moment I recalled some of the stories told on shipboard by European refugees bound for America.

We were silent on the trip except for a group of four University of California boys who were singing college songs. The bus crossed the Bay Bridge. Everyone stared at the beautiful view as if for the last time. The singing stopped.

AT about 12:30 we arrived at Tanforan Assembly Center. The gates were opened by military guards and the bus drove into the Tanforan Race Track grounds.

BAGGAGE of all sizes and shapes was piled high along the driveway in back of the grandstand, and earlier arrivals were searching among the stacks for their possessions. We waited in the parked bus for fifteen minutes; then the bus was driven around to the front of the grandstand.

THE soldier got out and opened the door and we filed out
past him.

MY brother and I were separated at this point. I was asked to sit on the bench with the women and wait while my brother lined up with the men and was searched from head to toe for contraband. Straight-edged razors, knives more than four inches long, and liquor were considered contraband.

MEDICAL examination followed. I was asked to enter one of the slightly partitioned and curtained compartments and was ordered to undress. A nurse looked into my mouth with a flashlight and checked my arms to see if I had been vaccinated for smallpox. When I rejoined my brother I asked him what they made him do. "They made us strip," he said.

AS head of the family I took the okayed slips from the nurse and presented them at the desk where rooms were being assigned. The girl who took the slips said, "Sorry, but we will have to send you and your brother to separate bachelor quarters. We are short of rooms for small fam- ily units." I told her that my brother and I had come as a family unit of two and that we intended to remain that way. I had to argue the point with each of the girls at the desk in turn, but finally they decided to let us remain as a family unit.

A guide was called to take us to our home, Barrack 16, Room 50. We went practically halfway around the race track and then diagonally across the center field through sticky mud and tall weeds. The ground was wet from the downpour of the day before. Those who had come on that day were drenched and their baggage was soaked. Friends who had entered the camp the previous week had warned us what camp was like so we came prepared with boots. When we arrived it was not raining, but now it started to sprinkle.

WE followed the guide past the race track to the other side where the horse stables were. We passed many stables before Stable 16 was pointed out to us. It was an isolated building surrounded by tall weeds and standing high above the ground. It was the only barrack with a raised walk and railing.

THE guide left us at the door of Stall 50. We walked in and dropped our things inside the entrance. The place was in semidarkness; light barely came through the dirty window on either side of the entrance. A swinging half-door divided the 20 by 9 ft. stall into two rooms. The roof sloped down from a height of twelve feet in the rear room to seven feet in the front room; below the rafters an open space extended the full length of the stable. The rear room had housed the horse and the front room the fodder. Both rooms showed signs of a hurried whitewashing. Spider webs, horse hair, and hay had been whitewashed with the walls. Huge spikes and nails stuck out all over the walls. A two-inch layer of dust covered the floor, but on removing it we discovered that linoleum the color of redwood had been placed over the rough manure-covered boards.

WE opened the folded spring cots lying on the floor of
the rear room and sat on them in the semidarkness. We
heard someone crying in the next stall.

IT was no use just sitting there, so we went to work cleaning the stall. We took turns sweeping the floor with a whisk broom. It was the only practical thing we had brought with us.

BY this time it was four o'clock and suppertime in camp. We rushed back to the huge grandstand. The ground floor served as the mess hall for the 5,000 evacuees then in the center; later it would serve 8,000. When we arrived, four lines, each a block long, waited outside the mess-hall doors. It was very windy and cold. An hour passed and we finally reached the door only to learn that the line did not lead anywhere. The thought of starting over again left us when we saw the length of the other lines. We decided to crowd ourselves in, as so many others were trying to do, but it was impossible. Everyone was hugging the person ahead. Fortunately we discovered a friend who made room for us. People glared at us as we squeezed into line.

AT the dishware and the silverware counter I picked up a plate, a knife, and a fork. I wiped my plate clean with my handkerchief and held it out to the first of the cooks, who was serving boiled potatoes with his hands. The second cook had just dished out the last of the canned Vienna sausages, the main part of the dinner, so I passed by him and received two slices of bread from a girl at the end of the food counter.

We were pushed into the mess hall, where the entire space was filled with long tables and backless benches. Each table was supposed to accommodate eight persons, but right now each was a bedlam of hungry people. We looked for an empty place but could find none. The air was stuffy and, having temporarily lost our appetites, we decided to forget about eating.

WE went in search of our belongings. Some of the baggage had been piled in the driveway at the entrance to the gates but most of it had been dumped in front of the grandstand. We climbed and fought our way through hundreds of crates, trunks, duffel bags, and cartons, but could not find our baggage. Truckloads were arriving about every two hours, so we decided our belongings would turn up later.

By this time the mess-hall line was short and we decided to try again. We managed to get some canned hash besides the potato and the two slices of bread. The mess hall had cleared to a great extent and the atmosphere was more pleasant. A pitcher of tea and a number of cups were on each table. We sat down to eat our first meal in the center.

WE carried our dirty dishes to the dishwashing counter. Groups of young fellows were removing the garbage with one hand and dipping the plates into a soapy mess with the other at a mass-production rate of speed. The cups and plates were thrown on racklike shelves to drain and dry.

AN enormous two-trailer Bekins Truck drove up as we left the mess hall. Lads who looked about sixteen years old were in charge of the unloading, and when the truck stopped they went to work. Packages and boxes came hurtling out; some of them split open as they hit the ground. My brother ran to the other side of the truck to watch for ours to appear. I was about to give up my vigil when suddenly he shouted, "Here they come!" I ran to join him just as he caught one of our suitcases. It was a cheap wooden one and could not take the beating; the cover was torn loose from the hinges.

WE collected our baggage and hailed a truck to have it delivered to our barrack. The truck was already bulging, but our belongings were tossed in, too, and we climbed on top and held on. On the long, bouncing ride back to the barrack we stopped to make several deliveries. At Barrack 16 we were unloaded with our goods. We dragged our stuff to our stall.

IT was now getting late in the evening, so we started on the half-mile walk back around the race track to get our mattresses. The mattress department was a stable filled with straw. We were given bags of ticking and were told to help ourselves to the straw. The few cotton mattresses available were reserved for the sick and the old.

WHEN we had finished filling the bags, the openings were sewed roughly together and we carried the bags away. It was very windy and dusty on the way back and we had some difficulty managing the awkward load.

FRIENDS who were there before us had advised us to
bring some foodstuffs, so we opened a can of peaches
and ate them with crackers.

WE shook the mattresses and flattened them out and made our beds with the sheets and blankets we had brought along. We "hit the hay" around ten that night, but learned very quickly that sleep was not to be easily won. Because the partitions were low and there were many holes in the boards they were made of, the crackling of the straw and the noises from the other stalls were incessant. Loud snores, the grinding of teeth, the wail of babies, the murmur of conversations—these could be heard the full length of the stable. Moreover, it was very cold and we were shivering. One blanket was not enough to keep us warm. We got up and opened the duffel bags and the suitcases and spread everything over our beds. Sleep finally overtook us around midnight. Thus ended our first day in the Tanforan Assembly Center.

THE camp was a mess.

IT was far from complete. Carpenters were working overtime building barracks in the center field. Additional washrooms, shower rooms, toilets, and laundry buildings were being planned and built throughout the camp.

THE first month was the hardest because adjustments had to be made to the new mode of life. The naked barracks and whitewashed stalls had to be fixed up into living quarters, and we had to get used to the lack of privacy of camp life.

As we had not brought our carpentry tools with us we had to send for them. While we waited for them to arrive, we searched the scrap-lumber piles for good pieces of wood. As more and more evacuees came into the center, the lumber piles shrank until they disappeared. Some of the people even went so far as to remove lumber from the unused horse stables, while the carpenters at work in the center field were having building materials snatched from under their noses.

EVERYONE was building furniture and fixing up barracks and stalls. Many of the discomforts of the camp were forgotten in this activity.

WOMEN, from grandmothers to toddlers, wore slacks or jeans.

EVACUEES were coming into the center at the rate of three hundred a day. The last group of 274 arrived from San Francisco on May 20, 1942. Every time a group arrived I went out to the grandstand to watch them go through the induction steps I had gone through a couple of weeks earlier. From the grandstand balcony I watched the coming and going of the baggage trucks.

The humor and pathos of the scenes made me decide to keep a record of camp life in sketches and drawings.

DURING the first month, typhoid and smallpox shots were given at a wholesale rate. Everyone had to have these vaccinations, while children had others besides. For nights we heard groans in the stable. Almost everyone was sick from the typhoid shots. The baby three stalls from us cried all the time. My brother, having started his inoculations before coming to camp, took his third and final shot. He complained that the final shot was meant for a horse.

THE vaccinations kept the medical staff busy. Evacuee
dentists, pharmacists, and optometrists assisted the few
doctors and nurses.

THE weather in Tanforan was fair. It was sunny on most days but always windy and dusty. My stall faced north and the sun never reached it. It was uncomfortable. I had a cold most of the time.

EVERY person leaving or entering the center was searched. No evacuee was permitted to leave the center except in case of emergency or death. Rules were very strict.

IN case of death, a rickety hearse arrived. Old men sitting in front of the hospital would watch and wonder, "When will my turn come?" Only immediate members of the family were permitted to attend the burial services, under armed guard.

CURFEW was imposed, and roll call was held every day at 6:45 A.M. and at 6:45 P.M. Each barrack had a house captain who made the rounds to check on us twice a day.

DAY and night Caucasian camp police walked their beats within the center. ("Caucasian" was the camp term for non-evacuee workers.) They were on the lookout for contraband and for suspicious actions.

THE Tanforan post office was one of the busiest places in the center. All packages were inspected. Many of them contained goods ordered from the indispensable Montgomery Ward, and Sears, Roebuck catalogs.

The infrequent letters from my father were always postmarked from a new camp in a different state. Letters from my European friends told me how lucky I was to be free and safe at home.

CHURCHES were early established to bolster the morale of the bewildered and humiliated people. There were Protestant, Catholic, Seventh Day Adventist, and Buddhist groups.

Another help to morale was the opportunity to work. Jobs of many kinds were open to able-bodied evacuee residents but employment was optional. Most of the adults worked.

At first we did not receive any wages and we did not know that we would get paid, but as time passed we were told that we would receive the rate of eight, twelve, and sixteen dollars per month for full-time work, depending on the type of work and the skill of the worker. In addition a clothing allowance credit of $3.75 per month was given each worker and his dependents, with allowances scaled down for children. The smallest of the first pay checks were for four cents; it cost ten cents to cash them.

NEARLY four hundred bachelors were housed in the grandstand "dorm." They slept and snored, dressed and undressed, in one continuous public performance. Some built "walls of Jericho" of sheets or blankets.

TO the older bachelors, life amounted to waiting for the next meal. Some creative souls finally found time to "develop" talents.

WHEN induction was over and the camp was somewhat
settled, the bachelors were moved from the grandstand
to Barrack 14 in our district.

THERE was a lack of privacy everywhere. The incomplete partitions in the stalls and the barracks made a single symphony of yours and your neighbors' loves, hates, and joys. One had to get used to snores, baby-crying, family troubles, and even to the jitterbugs.

ALTHOUGH cooking was not permitted in the barracks and stalls, blown fuses often left us in the darkness, guiltily pondering whether it was our hot plate or our neighbor's that did the trick.

WE had to make friends with the wild creatures in the
camp, especially the spiders, mice, and rats, because we
were outnumbered.

LAUNDRY buildings were conveniently set up in the different sections of the camp. Each building had three rooms: the laundry room, the ironing room, and the drying room. The one disadvantage of the laundry building was the continual lack of hot water.

My brother and I did our washing after midnight when we were sure of getting a washtub. There was no hot water at that hour, but we managed to haul it from the women's washroom a few barracks away. Our nocturnal visits used to annoy the laundry janitor.

MOST people preferred the sun-drying method to the protection from dust in the drying room in the laundry building.

Individual clotheslines were put up everywhere and anywhere. About a month before we left Tanforan the maintenance crew got around to putting up community lines for the different sections, but up to then the center looked like one of Rube Goldberg's creations.

AT first, the nearest washroom, shower, and latrine were located far away from us, on the other side of the race track. There were separate places for men and women, but confused men and women strayed into both places. The washrooms and the shower rooms were equipped for cold and hot water but the hot water was almost always used up, or the boiler had blown up during the night. Long tin troughs served as wash basins.

THE flush toilets were always out of commission. In the men's latrine the toilets were lined up in two rows back to back. In the women's the arrangement was the same, except that a half-partition separated the toilets conversationally in pairs. Later each toilet was separately partitioned.

EVERYONE liked to use the toilets in the grandstand where there was a little more privacy.

MANY of the women could not get used to the community toilets. They sought privacy by pinning up curtains and setting up boards.

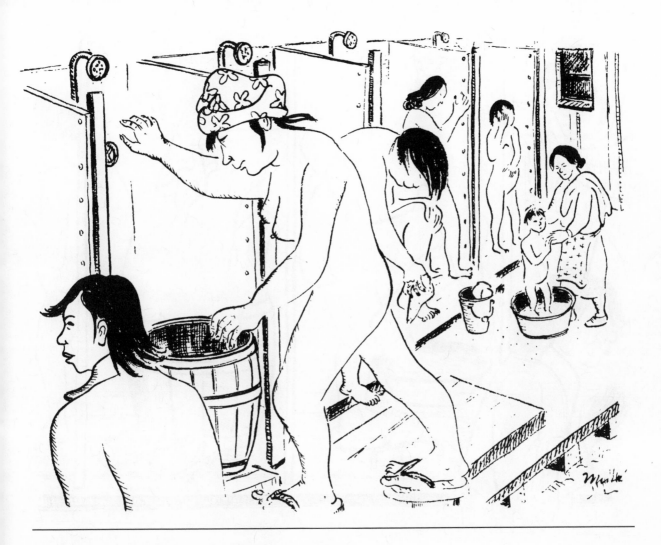

AT first the women were very self-conscious and timid
about using the showers.

The men's showers were in one large room but the
women's showers were slightly partitioned.

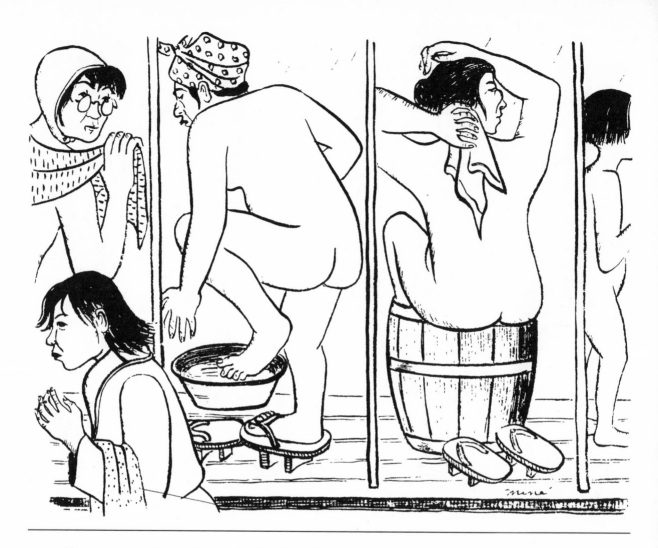

THE older women preferred the good old-fashioned bathtubs to showers. It was a common sight to see them bathing in pails, dishpans, or in tubs made from barrels.

FOR sanitary reasons, chlorine foot basins were placed at the entrance to each of the shower rooms. Most people were afraid to use this community foot bath and did acrobatic stunts to avoid it.

THE sewage system was poor. They were always digging up the camp to locate and fix the stoppages and leaks in the pipes. The stench from the stagnant sewage was terrible.

RESIDENTS were allowed to receive visitors in the grandstand from ten to twelve in the mornings and from one to four in the afternoons. The orders in the centers were strict, and much red tape was involved in getting a visitor's pass. The line of visitors was gaped at by passing motorists.

Friends often brought me food. One day a friend brought a Chinese meal, including my favorite egg-flower soup. After three hours of waiting in line he was finally admitted at the gate. He greeted me with a dripping carton. "Here is your egg flower—the soup is on my pants." After this I discouraged friends from bringing food. In fact I discouraged them from trying to visit me.

AT some of the centers, residents were allowed only to talk to visitors through a wire fence. At Tanforan a room on top of the grandstand was reserved for receiving visitors. Children under sixteen years of age were not allowed to visit the center. Pets that had been left behind with friends were also barred.

WE were close to freedom and yet far from it. The San Bruno streetcar line bordered the camp on the east and the main state highway on the south. Streams of cars passed by all day. Guard towers and barbed wire surrounded the entire center. Guards were on duty night and day.

A huge sign, "Enjoy Acme Beer," stood out like a beacon
on a nearby hill. The sign was clearly visible from every
section of the camp and was quite a joke to the thirsty
evacuees, especially on the warm days.

ON the barracks in the center field and on the stalls, ingenious family name plates and interesting signs were displayed with great pride. All signs in Japanese were ordered removed, but many fancy names, such as Inner Sanctum, Stall Inn, and Sea Biscuit, lent a touch of humor to the situation.

To discourage visitors, I nailed a quarantine sign on my door.

THE center had a canteen, but on most days there was
nothing to buy.

ON the days when there were goods for sale, practically
the whole camp turned out. It meant hours of waiting in
line and everything was rationed.

"LINE-UPS here and line-ups there" describes our daily
life. We lined up for mail, for checks, for meals, for showers, for washrooms, for laundry tubs, for toilets, for clinic
service, for movies. We lined up for everything.

MOTION pictures were shown weekly in the grandstand. Patrons brought blankets and pillows and sat on the floor. Those with folding chairs and stools were allowed to sit in the back.

One or two hours of waiting made no difference to the movie-conscious evacuees. Card-playing, knitting, reading, and gossiping passed the time away quickly, and often the cold was forgotten.

AT eight o'clock it was still daylight. The sun shone brightly into the room and made the moving picture dim and formless. The idea of going to a show made us happy, even if we could not see the picture. The entrance fee was our mess card. Different nights were reserved for a different group of mess halls.

WHEN the new mess halls were opened, residents were asked to bring their own plates and silverware and to wash them when the meal was finished. At first, washrooms and laundry tubs were used for the purpose; later, sinks were built at the exit to each of the mess halls so that people could wash their dishes as they left.

Table manners were forgotten. Guzzle, guzzle, guzzle; hurry, hurry, hurry. Family life was lacking. Everyone ate wherever he or she pleased. Mothers had lost all control over their children.

Before mess tickets were issued, most of us were hungry after one meal, so we would dash to another mess hall for a second meal. Some managed to get three meals this way.

IN the grandstand mess hall, even when no meal was in
progress, people sat around for hours.

IN Tanforan Assembly Center a movement for self-government was started by the evacuees. They organized a campaign complete with slogans and rallies to elect an official Center Advisory Council. The election gave the Issei their first chance to vote along with their citizen offspring. But army orders later limited self-government offices and votes to American citizens. To our disappointment, in August an army order dissolved all Assembly Center self-government bodies.

SCHOOLS were late in opening and difficult to organize because of the lack of buildings and necessary supplies. Volunteer evacuee teachers were used. Classroom discipline was poor. There were special adult classes in Americanization, history, sewing, art, and music. Preschools were very important in the center. Busy parents were assured that their children would have good care and good training. These schools were an effective counter-influence to the bad atmosphere of the camp.

In Tanforan I was an art instructor. I had elementary classes and college classes, and worked 44 hours a week for $16 a month.

THE library opened with sixty-five books. A great many
magazine and book donations came from "outside" to
help build a substantial library in the center.

RUMORS of all kinds were quickly picked up and quickly spread. One of the wildest was that the San Francisco Bay Bridge had been blown up.

ON a stroll around the track all kinds of amusing scenes
greeted us. Trying to forget, people occupied themselves
in games and sports or in just staring up at the sky.

ALTHOUGH idleness is a trait which the Japanese ordinarily will not tolerate, as the result of the demoralizing effect of center life we saw men lying around asleep in unusual places. I once came across a man perfectly at peace stretched out fast asleep on the top rail of the center-field fence. The lower grandstand floor was also an attractive spot for the sleepers.

IN front of almost all the stables and along the rows of barracks were planted victory gardens. Great care and attention were given to them by the owners, who were spurred by competitive pride. The best were those of former truck gardeners and nurserymen.

A group of landscape architects decided to build a lake to beautify the camp. Trees and shrubs were dug up from various places and transplanted in the center field. The size and location of a tree was no hindrance to trans- planting it if the tree fitted into the plan. The workmen struggled day after day with limited equipment. For a long time we were kept in wonderment by this activity. Everyone knew the camp was not a permanent one.

ON August 2, North Lake was formally opened. It had been transformed from a mere wet spot in the Tanforan scenery into a miniature aquatic park, complete with bridge, promenade, and islands. The lake was a great joy to the residents and presented new material for the artists. In the morning sunlight and at sunset it added great beauty to the bleak barracks.

THE fountain and pond on the south side of the center field was one of the most active sport areas in the camp. In homemade sailboats the enthusiasts displayed their craftsmanship and their skill as sailors. A former fisherman invented a sailboat out of a telephone pole and took children on as passengers.

THE residents spent much of their time on the grandstand. The panorama from there reminded them of the hills of home. One had the whole view of the race track and the surrounding country. Trains passed back and forth in the distance and airplanes skimmed overhead.

People came to bask in the sun in the wind-protected privacy of the grandstand booths; others came for a private dice game. Some came to meditate, and there were those who came to sleep.

MOST of the center's events took place in front of or in the grandstand—talent shows, pageants, and dances. As a grand finale before leaving Tanforan we held a four-day Mardi Gras and a gay parade.

GAMBLING was prohibited but at the beginning of the
center's existence there were raids and arrests. The
prowling camp police squelched some games.

KNITTING was a great pastime for the womenfolks. It was also taken up by some of the young men, who would knit themselves socks, mittens, caps, and sweaters. One had knitted a complete outfit of skirt and jacket for his mother, but he never displayed his skill to the public for fear that the girls would laugh at him.

GOH and *shogi*, Japanese games somewhat similar to our chess and checkers, were great pastimes for the Issei menfolk. A recreation hall was set aside for these games, but private games were also held throughout the camp. Important tournaments and matches took place frequently. Interest was so great that children learned to play, and sometimes beat their grandparents.

ON warm days it was unbearable in the stalls and barracks. The stench of manure returned with the heat, and
this in turn brought back the horseflies. Most of the people remained outdoors on such days, and usually I did,
too, but there were times when I kept on working inside.

Later, by the order of the medical authority, all windows
in the stalls were hinged so that they could be opened.

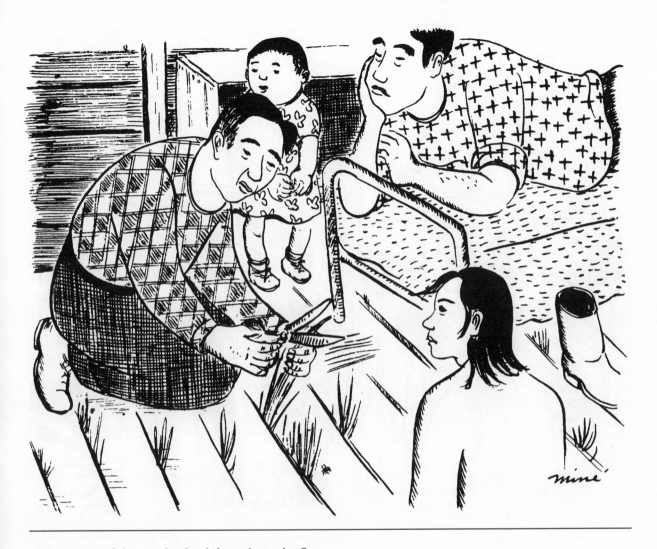

THE warping of the new lumber left cracks in the floor
half an inch to an inch wide. Through the cracks the tall
grass came up.

THERE were two center-wide inspections at Tanforan. The first, on instructions from the Wartime Civil Control Administration in San Francisco, was entirely routine; it was made because the evacuees' baggage had not been thoroughly searched upon arrival. Potentially dangerous tools, such as saws and chisels, were confiscated, and Japanese phonograph records and literature were also taken away. (Bibles and religious books were later returned.)

The second inspection was conducted by the army. At this time a still more thorough search was made. Each section was placed under guard while the search was conducted. Because of the quarantine sign on my door they almost passed me by.

We inferred from the inspections that we would be moved to a permanent center fairly soon.

RUMORS about the site and date and conditions of the relocation were always arising in Tanforan to make a brief stir among the residents. But in August, relocation assumed the shape of reality in the minds of all.

Posts strung with chicken-wire appeared on the northeast corner of the camp near the back gate by the railroad siding. The entire area around the gate, including the laundry building and the toilets, was completely fenced off, leaving one section open.

Although there was no official word on specific details, residents were putting two and two together and arriving at the same conclusion—that we were going to a relocation center in Utah. These relocation centers, ten in all, were under the War Relocation Authority, which superseded the Wartime Civil Control Administration.

AS the time for moving drew nearer, the administration announced that individual residents might leave the center under police guard to make final settlements concerning business and personal property.

I was granted permission to check personal belongings that were stored in a private home in Berkeley. I received a notice telling me to report at 8:00 A.M. at the main gate. After I had filled out numerous forms a Caucasian police was assigned to me. He was responsible for my return by 4:30 P.M. and I was responsible for his travel and lunch expenses.

That one day of liberty was wonderful. I was like a child. I wanted to buy everything.

THE center-wide inspections had been held; there were now administration bulletins on such matters as baggage preparation, the approximate dates of the movement out of Tanforan, and conduct on trains. No one knew exactly when and where the relocation would begin, but it was not long before we received a notice telling us to be packed and ready by the 16th of September. Barracks 16 and 14 were listed in the first group.

EVERYWHERE there was a stir of final preparation, of packing and crating. Scrap-lumber furniture and shelves had to come down and the precious tags bearing the family identification number had to be brought out of safekeeping.

Two days before the date of departure everything had to be packed and tagged and ready for inspection. Immediately after inspection, each box, crate, and duffel bag was closed and taken away.

On September 9, 1942, the advance work group of 214 people left for the Central Utah Relocation Project to make preparations for induction.

ON the 16th of September at five in the afternoon, my brother and I reported with our hand luggage to a newly constructed bull pen. We were assigned to Group 5, Section 8. Our train captain read off the names in the group and told us to seat ourselves accordingly, 45 to 50 people in each group.

At the gate, a Caucasian worker checked our names and family number and told us to open our luggage for inspection. Thousands of people, most of them friends of the departing residents, were gathered around the wire fence to bid us good-bye.

INSIDE the laundry building, also used as a bull pen, long
wooden benches separated the rooms into sections.

OTHER groups came in and were likewise seated, each in its respective section, until all the groups for this trip were accounted for. Half an hour later the parade to the train started. A cheering crowd of remaining evacuees and a group of armed military police lined up on either side of the path leading to the train.

WITH about five hundred evacuees and fifty military police on board, the train started on its way at exactly 7:45 P.M. Our last glimpse of Tanforan Assembly Center brought smiles. Some of the residents had climbed to the stable roofs and were holding aloft huge bon voyage signs, as others waved good-bye to us.

THE trip was a nightmare that lasted two nights and a day. The train creaked with age. It was covered with dust, and as the gaslights failed to function properly we traveled in complete darkness most of the night, reminding me of the blackout trains in Europe. All shades were drawn and we were not allowed to look out of the windows.

For many it was the first long journey. They were both excited and sad to leave California and the Bay region. To this day for many of them, the world is as large as from San Francisco to Tanforan to Topaz.

The first night was a novelty after four and a half months of internment. However, I could not sleep and I spent the entire night taking the chair apart and re-adjusting it. Many became train sick and vomited. The children cried from restlessness. At one point on the way, a brick was thrown into one of the cars. The journey was otherwise uneventful. In the daytime we saw only barren desert lands of Nevada and Utah; for we had passed the beauty spots of California during the night.

I could forgive all other discomforts because of oranges and lemons. Boxes of them were set out in each of the coaches for the passengers. It was a precaution against illness on the train. The older people did not care for them, so I ate their share too.

The meals on the train were good after camp fare.

IN the late afternoon the train stopped in the desert
somewhere in northern Nevada and for half an hour
we were permitted to get off the train and walk around.
Barbed-wire fences bounded the stretch on either side of
the track and military police stood on guard every fifteen
feet.

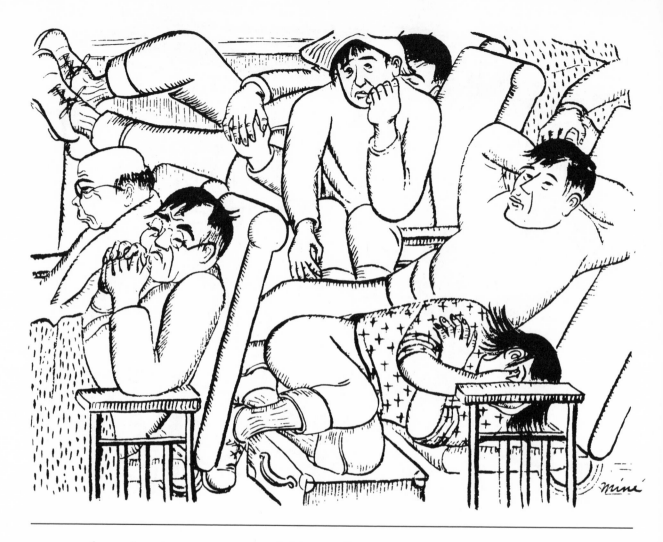

RESTLESS from exhaustion, everyone was wakeful on the second night. Nothing functioned well on this old relic. The steam heat could not be turned off, so the car was overheated and stuffy. About two o'clock in the morning someone shouted, "The Great Salt Lake!" There was a general scramble to open the windows and look out. It was pitch black and I could see nothing, but I could hear the ripple of the water. An hour later the train pulled into the huge railroad station at Ogden. I have a dim rec-ollection of seeing ice and water put on the train, but do not know how long we stopped here.

I was half awake when the train arrived at Salt Lake City. A small group of Japanese Americans had come to see their friends on the train. The big clock in the station indicated that it was already 4 A.M. We tried to sleep the rest of the morning.

THE train arrived in Delta at eight o'clock, but we were all too tired to be excited. The captain of our car was fast asleep. Officials were darting about and there was some commotion. The Chief of Project Reports at Topaz came on board the train and handed to each of us the first copy of the Topaz *Times*. We chuckled as we read, "Topaz, the Jewel of the Desert." The paper described the camp and gave instructions to the newcomers.

By this time the car captain was awake and was calling us to attention. We stepped out of the train and into the bus waiting alongside. Military police were on guard. When the bus was full, one of them got into the front seat. The driver stepped on the gas and the bus moved off.

WE rode through seventeen miles of alfalfa fields and greasewood-covered desert. Half of the distance was made over rough, newly constructed dirt roads. We were all eyes, hoping to spot something interesting in the flat, dry land which extended for miles in all directions. Suddenly, the Central Utah Relocation Project was stretched out before us in a cloud of dust. It was a desolate scene. Hundreds of low black barracks covered with tarred paper were lined up row after row. A few telephone poles stood like sentinels, and soldiers could be seen patrolling the grounds.

THE bus struggled through the soft alkaline dirt, past the white administration barracks and the black resident barracks to Block 4 Mess Hall. This, together with the laundry building, was the induction center for the day. As we stepped out of the bus, we could hear band music and people cheering, but it was impossible to see anything through the dust. The band was a group of former Boy Scouts from Berkeley. When we finally battled our way into the safety of the building we looked as if we had fallen into a flour barrel.

INSIDE the hall, the inductors, men and women, were seated along the inner side of mess tables arranged in the shape of a horseshoe. A room was now assigned to each family. We discovered that there were six rooms to a barrack, 12 barracks to a block. Every block had its own mess hall, recreation hall, and combination laundry, showers, and toilets.

WE took our assignment (Block 7, Barrack 11, Room F) and proceeded to the laundry building, passing down a roped-off section between lines of cheering people. We were worn out and blurry-eyed.

AS we passed through the laundry, a Caucasian nurse peered into our throats with a flashlight and gave us the okay slips. We were now free to go in search of our room.

THREE girls whom we knew offered to take us to 7-11-F.
The wind was playing havoc with the fine dust particles.

F was one of the end rooms. It was a large rectangle (about 20 by 10 ft.) and completely bare, furnished only with a ceiling light and a closet space near the door. There were two windows to the north and one to the south. A three-inch layer of alkali dust covered the masonite floor. The room was unfinished, the bare wall beams and rafters giving it a skeletonlike appearance.

When we went to Mess 7 for lunch we found a dining hall set for about three hundred people. It had a pleasanter atmosphere than the dining halls in Tanforan. Our first meal was served semifamily style, and it was good. As we glanced around we saw only bachelors. Few of our Tanforan friends were there.

We were not happy with our neighborhood, and

immediately after lunch we went to the housing staff to see if another room could be assigned to us. In the ensuing arguments we not only failed to have our room changed, but ended by receiving a new member into the family. We were now three instead of two. End rooms like ours were designed for three, so we invited a young California student to come in with us. We chose him because he was expecting to join his father in another camp as soon as the transfer papers came through.

Army cots were provided as in Tanforan Assembly Center. They were stacked in convenient places in each of the blocks. We brought home three.

TICK bags were given to us again. However, this time we did not have to wait long to have them exchanged for cotton mattresses.

TWO army blankets were distributed to each of us.

THE boys used two of the blankets to curtain off a room
for me in one corner.

OUR baggage was misplaced. We must have looked
through a thousand pieces before we found it.

TOPAZ, the Central Utah Project, was a more or less permanent center. Therefore, the evacuees looked for work immediately upon induction. Everyone wanted a job for which he had been trained or had some skill. The three of us were accepted for work on the Topaz *Times*, at the professional rate of $19 a month, with an additional credit of $3.75 for clothing. The other rates of pay in the center were $12 and $16.

Our newspaper kept the residents informed about the center and the outside. Originally a mimeographed sheet issued three times a week, it later became a daily, with a Japanese section and a comic section. All news passed the censorship of the administration staff.

After two months with the Topaz *Times*, a small group of us decided to break away and start a fifty-page art and literary magazine. We called it *Trek*. Three issues appeared.

THE camp was only two-thirds finished. A contractor's crew of about a hundred was stationed in Block 1. Fences and watch towers were not yet constructed, but soldiers patrolled the camp and the uncompleted sections.

The entire Topaz project area occupied 17,500 acres. The center contained 42 city blocks, of which 36 comprised the residential area, one square mile in extent. At first we were not permitted beyond it, but later we could wander to the rest of the area.

ALL residential blocks looked alike; people were lost all
the time.

COMFORT was uppermost in the minds of the people. All were on the lookout for building material for partitions and furniture. Lumber and sheet-rock boards were scarce and well guarded, but since building material was not furnished to the residents as promised, they became desperate. With the passing of time and the coming of cold weather, stealing no longer became a crime but an act of necessity. Everybody was out to get building material. There were guards everywhere, but the residents became skillful at dodging them; worried mothers were the most skillful of all.

The deep, open ditches for the sewer pipes were the chief hazard after dark. Our nocturnal excursions in search of lumber were made in the pitch dark; a few scattered lights indicated the location of the administrative buildings and the main roads.

From the lumber thus borrowed from the government we partitioned our large room into three small sections, and made tables, benches, and rough chairs.

THERE was no privacy in our one-room home. People came and went. Bull sessions lasted all day and far into the night. We were tired of the shiftless existence and were restless.

A feeling of uncertainty hung over the camp; we were worried about the future. Plans were made and remade, as we tried to decide what to do. Some were ready to risk anything to get away. Others feared to leave the protection of the camp.

THOSE who wished privacy went out into the wide open spaces.

THE precious scrap-lumber piles were guarded night and day, but in the zero weather the guards burned up most of it in order to keep themselves warm. What was left was carefully divided among the residents by the block managers.

AT first it was impossible to drink the water because of the strong taste from the chlorine and the pipes. Thirsty people went to the one well with good water, near the U.S. Engineer's Office, until this was condemned as contaminated. Some braver souls managed to go into the prohibited area to the Caucasian workers' canteen. There were times when we felt like prospectors lost in the middle of the desert. (Whether due to the water or the food, there were occasional epidemics of dysentery.)

THE clanging of thirty-six makeshift iron bells indicated chowtime in camp. There was the usual line-up and the slow-moving procession to the food counter. Unlike Tanforan, dishes and silverware were provided. The main course was served at the counter and tea was served at the table by the waiters. Side dishes were placed on the tables.

Each mess hall fed from two hundred and fifty to three hundred persons. Food was rationed, as it was for the civilian population on the outside. The allowance for food varied from 31 cents to 45 cents a day per person. Often a meal consisted of rice, bread, and macaroni, or beans, bread, and spaghetti. At one time we were served liver for several weeks, until we went on strike.

ABOUT five hundred arrivals from Tanforan were inducted every other day.

On October 6, 1942, 550 former San Franciscans from
Santa Anita Assembly Center arrived. The final contingent of 308 people came from Tanforan on October 15.
The Boy Scout band welcomed each incoming bus, and
there were welcome signs for the new residents.

Mass meetings of welcome were held at the different mess halls. The project director and other officials,
including the drum and bugle corps, were on hand to give
each new group an impressive showing.

THE first snow fell in Topaz on October 13. The residents
went wild with excitement; for most of them this was the
first experience of snow.

EACH family was given a pot-bellied stove. Ours was
moved in with me.

ON cold days the stove centralized the family gatherings.

THE snow melted quickly and, as the alkaline soil did not
absorb water, the ground became a sticky mass of mud.

HARDY trees and shrubs were brought from the distant mountains and transplanted throughout the camp. It was doubtful that anything would grow in this alkaline soil but to our surprise, in the following spring, green began to appear in the trees and the shrubs, especially on those planted near the washrooms.

IN November, Arbor Day was celebrated by the distribution of small shrubs to each block. There was an overnight change in camp scenery. Trees and shrubs appeared in the most unexpected places.

WHEN the cold days came, the War Relocation Authority distributed G.I. clothes to all those employed, both
women and men. It was welcome if peculiar apparel—
warm pea jackets and army uniforms, sizes 38 and 44,
apparently left over from the first World War.

IN Tanforan we had ordered our clothing allotment from
the Sears, Roebuck summer catalog. These clothes, with
many substitutions, now began to arrive.

EVERYONE was dressed alike, because of the catalog
orders and the G.I. clothes.

THE "winterization" of buildings began when we first
arrived in camp, with the administration buildings, mess
halls, and schools. In the homes it began just before
Christmas. We all helped to hurry the work because we
were anxious to unpack and fix up our living quarters.

FENCE posts and watch towers were now constructed
around the camp by the evacuees to fence themselves in.

THE first Christmas was sad. The mess halls provided decorated trees and served special dinners but there was a lack of holiday spirit. Some families made a brave attempt to hold their usual celebrations.

The *Trek* staff held a party. We concocted a drink of grape jam and lemons and pretended that it was the real stuff. Dancing and games made the party a noisy affair.

MOCHI-MAKING added a little more gaiety on New Year's Day. *Mochi* is made to celebrate the traditional Japanese New Year. To make it, a special kind of rice is boiled and pounded with wooden mallets into a sticky mass from which round cakes are molded. Much jovial ceremony is connected with *mochi*-making.

AN ice rink was constructed on the south side of the camp, and on cold days skating was a good sport. However, in Topaz the season was very short.

EACH block had a laundry complete with washboards and clotheslines. Much time was spent in the laundry. There was plenty of hot water and the alkaline water made washing easy.

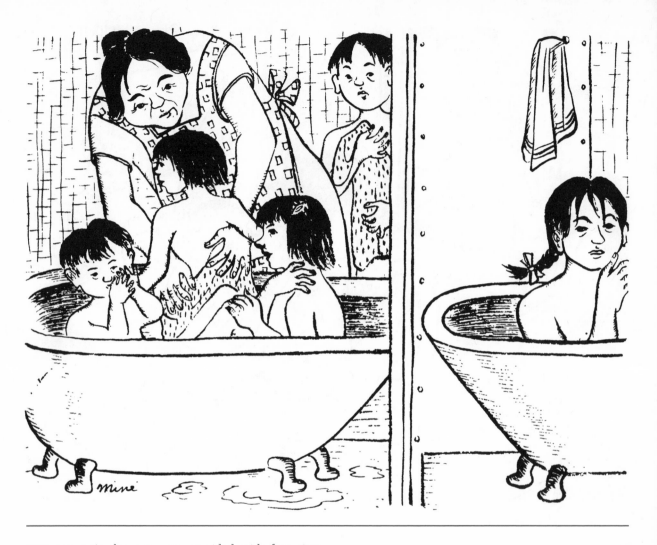

THE women's showers were provided with four tiny bathtubs. Later the desperate old men repartitioned the walls so that one of the tubs was on their side of the shower room.

THERE was a morning and evening rush to and from the washroom, of people in *getas* (traditional wooden clogs), in underwear, in nightgowns, and in robes. Homemade *getas* took the place of rationed shoes and boots. Because of the mud puddles, some people built their *getas* a foot high.

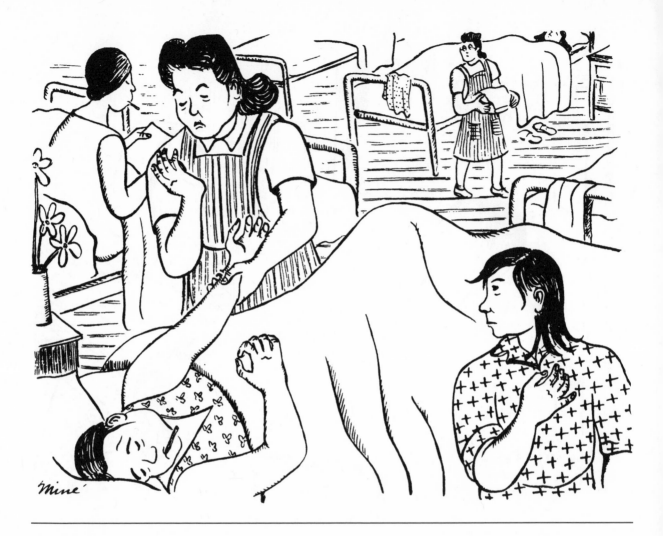

THE army-type hospital had 175 beds. It was directed by Caucasians but was staffed largely by evacuee doctors, dentists, and nurses.

The dead were sent to Salt Lake City for cremation, and the ashes were held for burial until the day of return to the Bay region. The cemetery at the far end of the camp was never used.

THE birth rate in the center was high.

A community cooperative was established. It provided a canteen, dry-goods store, beauty parlor, barber shop, cleaning establishment, shoe repair shop, and movies. Discounts were given and refunds were made to the members.

The canteen was like a country store where people gathered to discuss family and community problems. There the rumors of the day were circulated and notes exchanged on many subjects.

AS in Tanforan, education was stressed. There were three
nursery schools in Topaz.

SCHOOL organization was an improvement over Tan-foran. The curriculum followed the requirements of the state of Utah and the school was staffed by Caucasian teachers and by teachers selected from among the evac-uees; the latter received only the standard camp wages.

AMERICANIZATION classes were organized and were
held every night for the Issei.

THE first mass gathering in Topaz was a memorial service to honor a Japanese American soldier who died while in service. All faiths were represented, and former members of the American Legion also participated.

ART and hobby shows were of great interest. The residents exhibited vases and desk sets of wood, toys, stuffed animals and dolls, garments and knitted ware, carvings of stone and wood, finger rings of cellophane or fashioned from toothbrush handles, peach seeds or beads, tools made of scrap iron, and beautiful hats made of citrus-fruit wrappings woven with potato-sack strings. Ingenious use was made of everything that could be found in the center.

RECREATION halls had for equipment only what the evacuees were able to provide. Ping pong, badminton, and cards were the important indoor games. Basketball, tennis, golf, football, and baseball were the outdoor games—baseball was the favorite sport.

SUMO performances were given for those interested in the old sports of Japan.

KITE-MAKING and flying was not limited to the young-sters.

ENTERTAINMENTS were given on makeshift stages in the mess halls and in the open. Talent shows and plays were presented. Later an auditorium was built.

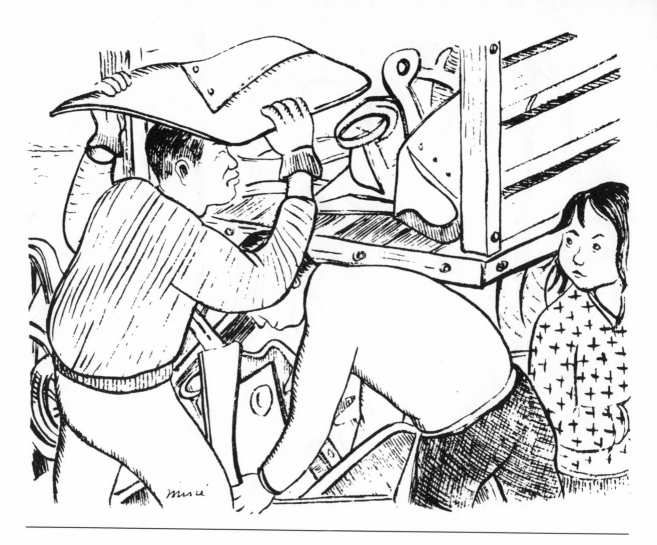

THERE were scrap-metal drives, bond sales, Red Cross
drives, and blood donations to help us keep up with the
outside world.

ON January 29, 1943, President Roosevelt announced that volunteers would be accepted in a Japanese American combat unit. A recruiting team came to the center, and a printed form was submitted to all men of military age. It contained 28 questions to determine loyalty and willingness to fight. Question 28 read: "Will you swear unqualified allegiance to the United States of America and forswear any form of allegiance or obedience to the Japanese Emperor or any other foreign power or organization?"

At the same time, the War Relocation Authority, yielding to increasing pressure, decided to conduct a general registration of all persons in the camp seventeen years of age or older. To determine their loyalty, Question 28 was used. It brought about a dilemma. Aliens (Issei) would be in a difficult position if they renounced Japanese citizenship and thereby made themselves stateless persons. Many of the Nisei also resented the question because of the assumption that their loyalty might be divided; it was confusing that their loyalty to the United States should be questioned at the moment when the army was asking them to volunteer.

The registration form was long and complicated. The questions were difficult to understand and answer. Center-wide meetings were held, and the anti-administration rabble rousers skillfully fanned the misunderstandings.

STRONGLY pro-Japanese leaders in the camp won over the fence-sitters and tried to intimidate the rest. In the end, however, everybody registered. On the basis of the answers (plus further investigation by the Federal Bureau of Investigation), the "disloyal" were finally weeded out for eventual segregation and the "loyal" were later granted "leave clearance"—the right to leave camp, find a job, and "relocate."

DESPITE the registration misunderstandings and the threats, 105 young men were accepted for service in the Japanese American Combat Team, out of the many—including aliens—who volunteered. Our university friend was one of the 105.

THE excitement of registration had just begun to subside when 230 evacuees from Hawaii arrived to take up residence in Block 1. The travel-weary people were greeted with cold Topazian stares. Even the welcoming notes of a small band died away as the pathetic procession alighted from army trucks. The men looked like turtles in their outsize khaki coats. The bright leis around their necks gave the scene an incongruously festive air. There were few women and children in the group.

A few weeks later the Wakasa case stirred up the center. An elderly resident was shot and killed within the center area inside the fence, by a guard in one of the watch-towers. Particulars and facts of the matter were never satisfactorily disclosed to the residents. The anti-administration leaders again started to howl and the rest of the residents shouted for protection against soldiers with guns. As a result, the guards were later removed to the rim of the outer project area and firearms were banned.

AN impressive memorial service was held for the unfortunate victim. The women of each block made enormous floral wreaths with paper flowers.

THEN Easter came. A large outdoor ceremony was planned but the elements foiled the plans. Everyone anticipated a grand ceremony and put on their Sunday best. At the last strains of the "Hosanna," an unusually violent wind and dust storm struck the center. People ran in all directions for shelter.

IN spring the climate in Topaz was mild. The days were warm and the nights cool. The extremes of temperature ranged from 106 degrees in summer to 30 degrees below in winter. The rainfall averaged 8 inches. But the wind blew from all points of the compass most of the time.

THEY tried everything to control the wind and the dust. They plowed the empty areas, made irrigation ditches, and spread gravel between the barracks. But nothing was successful; the elements won out.

THE sewage swamp was located half a mile directly west of the center. Despite the purification system, the stench came sailing into camp whenever the wind was in the right direction.

TEMPORARY leaves were granted to volunteer seasonal workers. They were the first to be allowed to leave the project area. The first groups left to pick beets and fruit; turkey-plucking and other jobs followed, and many more groups went out.

THE Buddhists held an impressive parade and folk dances to celebrate *Hanamatsuri* (a Flower Festival) on the anniversary of the birth of Buddha.

THERE were 150 in the first high-school graduation class. Rented blue caps and gowns added much color to the large outdoor ceremony. The graduates were very serious.

IN the summer in Topaz we had a choice of being eaten by mosquitoes outdoors or suffocating with the heat indoors. There was no way to get rid of the mosquitoes; the entire area was a breeding ground for them because of the non-absorbent alkaline soil.

THE warm summer days brought all kinds of insects besides mosquitoes. The distribution of screens to all of the families finally kept the pests out of our rooms.

WHEN the hot weather came to Topaz, 4,000 straw hats were sold in a day.

DESPITE reports that the alkaline soil was not good for agricultural purposes, in the spring practically everyone set up a victory garden. Some of the gardens were organized, but most of them were set up anywhere and any way. Makeshift screens were fashioned out of precious cardboard boxes, cartons, and scraps of lumber to protect the plants from the whipping dust storms.

IN the evening there was the usual bucket brigade from
the laundry buildings to the gardens.

DOGS and cats were common in the center. Most of the dogs were of odd mongrel combinations and had short, sawed-off legs. In a year's time the number increased to the point that the administration had to compel the licensing of all dogs.

RESIDENTS began to keep domesticated and wild animals and birds. Block 41 even started a zoo. It was finally necessary for the administration and the medical authorities to put a stop to the practice.

TO provide enough meat and fresh vegetables, a variety of vegetables was produced on the project farms and the agricultural division raised cattle, chickens, and hogs.

The hogs ate everything we left, and ultimately we ate the hogs.

AT harvest time everyone pitched in to help.

IN September, 1943, on the first anniversary of Topaz, the camp looked somewhat as it had in the beginning. Because of the strongly alkaline soil and the poor quality of the pipes, the entire water and sewage system had to be dug up and the pipes changed. At first the plumbing crew tried to fix the leaks but they could not keep up with them.

THE program of segregation was now instituted. One of its purposes was to protect loyal Japanese Americans from the continuing threats of pro-Japanese agitators. Tule Lake, one of the ten original centers, was chosen as the segregation center for the disloyal. In the fall of 1943 thirteen hundred Topazians (about one tenth of the total) were sent there. The group included all who had said they wished to return to Japan; the "No, nos," that is, those who would not change their unsatisfactory answers to the questionnaire when they were given a chance to do so; all who remained under suspicion of disloyalty after investigation by the War Relocation Authority and the Federal Bureau of Investigation; and close relatives who would rather be segregated with their families than be separated from them.

Whatever decision was made, families suffered deeply. Children had to go to Tule Lake with their parents, but some adolescents resented the label "disloyal" and fought bitterly to remain behind.

TWELVE hundred loyal citizens and aliens were transferred from Tule Lake to Topaz. Their arrival once more
brought excitement to our now relatively peaceful city.

THE rules were becoming much less rigid. Block shopping was introduced, whereby a resident of each block was permitted to shop in the nearby town of Delta for the rest of the block. Special permits were arranged ahead of time by the administration. There was a thorough inspection by the military police both on leaving and returning.

UNDER the change in rules, many now went outside the fences to the outer project area to gather vegetation and small stones for their gardens. Others hunted for arrow heads.

MANY went fishing in the irrigation ditches, about three miles away on the outskirts of the project agricultural area.

RELOCATION programs were finally set up in the center to return residents to normal life. Students had led the way by going out to continue their education in the colleges and universities willing to accept them. Seasonal workers followed, to relieve the farm labor shortage.

Many volunteered for the army. Government jobs opened up, and the defense plants claimed others. The Intelligence Division of the army and navy demanded still others as instructors and students. My brother had left in June to work in a wax-paper factory in Chicago. Later he was inducted into the army.

Much red tape was involved, and "relocatees" were checked and double checked and rechecked. Citizens were asked to swear unqualified allegiance to the United

States and to defend it faithfully from all foreign powers. Aliens were asked to swear to abide by the laws of the United States and to do nothing to interfere with the war effort. Jobs were checked by the War Relocation offices and even the place of destination was investigated before an evacuee left.

In January of 1944, having finished my documentary sketches of camp life, I finally decided to leave.

AFTER plowing through the red tape, through the madness of packing again, I attended forums on "How to Make Friends" and "How to Behave in the Outside World."

I was photographed.

THE day of my departure arrived. I dashed to the block manager's office to turn in the blankets and other articles loaned to me, and went to the Administration Office to secure signatures on the various forms given me the day before. I received a train ticket and $25, plus $3 a day for meals while traveling; these were given to each person relocating on an indefinite permit. I received four typewritten cards to be filled out and returned after relocation, and a booklet, "When You Leave the Relocation Center," which I was to read on the train.

I dashed to the mess hall for a bite to eat, then to the Administration Office, picked up my pass and ration book at the Internal Security Office, and hurried to the gate. There I shook hands with the friends who had gathered to see me off. I lined up to be checked by the WRA and the army.

I was now *free*.

I looked at the crowd at the gate. Only the very old or very young were left. Here I was, alone, with no family responsibilities, and yet fear had chained me to the camp. I thought, "My God! How do they expect those poor people to leave the one place they can call home." I swallowed a lump in my throat as I waved good-bye to them.

I entered the bus. As soon as all the passengers had been accounted for, we were on our way. I relived momentarily the sorrows and the joys of my whole evacuation experience, until the barracks faded away into the distance. There was only the desert now. My thoughts shifted from the past to the future.